C000171667

The Waterways of Lincoln and Boston

- The Fossdyke
- River Witham
- Witham Navigable Drains
- Slea Navigation
- Horncastle Canal

Christine Richardson and John Lower

The Hallamshire Press

A Richlow Guide

Text © 1997 Interleaf Productions Limited
Photographs and Maps © 1997 John Lower and Christine Richardson

Published by The Hallamshire Press
The Hallamshire Press is an imprint of
Interleaf Productions Limited
Broom Hall
Sheffield S10 2DR
England

Typeset by Interleaf Productions Limited
Printed in Singapore

British Library Cataloguing in Publication Data

   A catalogue record for this book is available from the British Library

ISBN 1-874718-172

Contents

Acknowledgements

We wish to thank the many people who have helped with information for this guide, including Dave Carnell, John Baylis, and Mick and Carol Golds (Inland Waterways Association), Pat Taylor and David Turner (Sleaford Navigation Society), Andrew Dawson (British Waterways) and Ken Barber (Witham FIDB).

Cover photograph: The River Witham, Lincoln

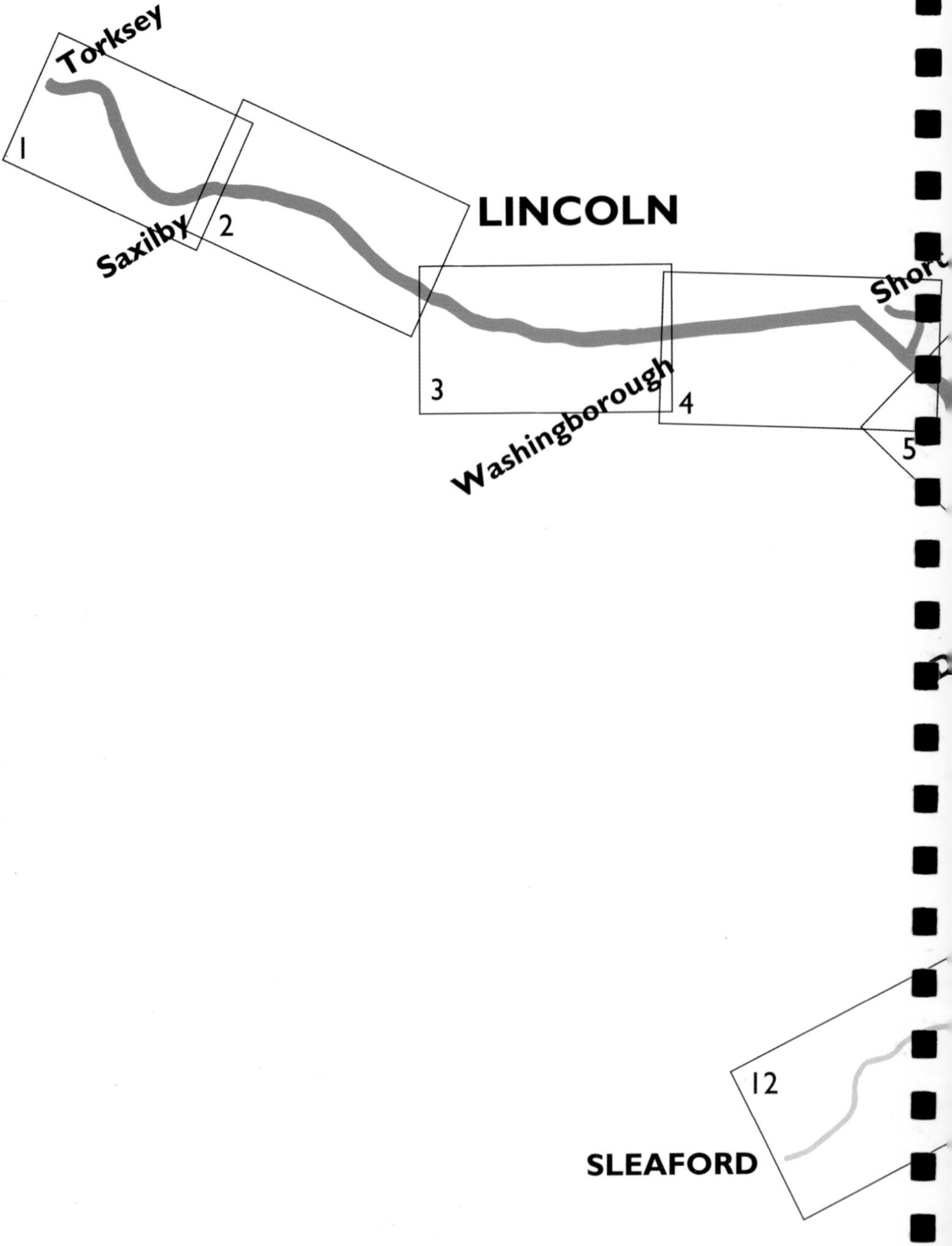

Torksey

1

Saxilby

2

LINCOLN

3

Washingborough

4

Short

5

12

SLEAFORD

4

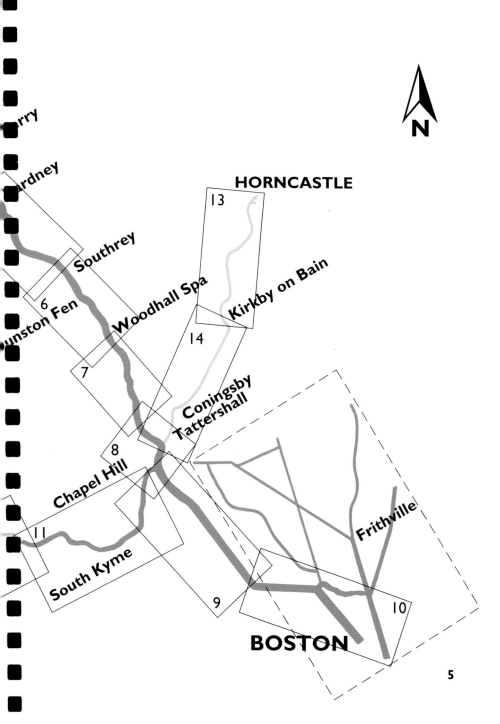

rry

rdney

HORNCASTLE

13

Southrey

6

nston Fen

Woodhall Spa

Kirkby on Bain

14

7

Coningsby
Tattershall

8

Chapel Hill

11

South Kyme

9

Frithville

10

BOSTON

Distances (in miles)

Fossdyke/Witham

Torksey										
5½	Saxilby									
11	5½	Lincoln								
13½	8	2½	Washingborough							
20½	15	9½	7	Bardney						
23½	18	12½	10	3	Dunston Fen					
27	21½	16	13½	6½	3½	Kirkstead Bridge				
31	25½	20	17½	10½	7½	4	Tattershall Bridge			
33	27½	22	19½	12½	9½	6	2	Chapel Hill		
40½	35	29½	27	20	17	13½	9½	7½	Anton's Gowt	
43	37½	32	29½	22½	19½	16	12	10	2½	Boston

Slea

Chapel Hill		
7½	Cobblers Lock	
12	4½	Sleaford

Horncastle

Horncastle		
5½	Kirkby	
11	5½	Dogdyke

Key to Maps

CP = Car Park
FC = Fish & Chip Shop
GP = Garage (Fuel)
GS = General Store
LB = Letter Box
PH = Public House
PO = Post Office
R = Restaurant
T = Telephone
WC = Public Toilet

━━━ Railway and Station

+ — + Disused Railway

------- Public Footpath

Viking Way

✝ Church

△ Triangulation Point

━━━ Navigable Waterway

▬▬▬ Non-navigable Waterway

▬) Lock

↰ Turning Place

- - - Towpath

M72 = Moorings
(Number indicates maximum stay permitted in hours)

MS = Milestone
RD = Rubbish Disposal
W = Water Point

Introduction

This is a guide to the central waterways of Lincolnshire for all visitors. The area it covers is mostly rural, with large skies and mind-unwinding peace.

The city of Lincoln provides many highlights, and Boston, Sleaford, Horncastle, and Woodhall Spa have charms of their own. As do the smaller villages.

Coverage is of the rivers Witham, Slea, and Bain, as well as the Fossdyke, the Horncastle Canal, and the remote navigable channels near Boston.

In its near-100 pages there are:-

- Clear maps, and full colour illustrations.
- Full navigational details for boaters, including access details from the Trent and the Wash.
- Practical information for walkers, cyclists, anglers and road visitors.
- Visitor attractions in the area.
- The history of the waterways and the local areas.
- The wildlife that may be seen.

The authors are local enthusiasts who have explored the waterways by boat, foot, cycle and road. They have written many waterway books including two other Richlow guides. They are also regular contributors to national magazines.

Care should always be taken at deep water locations such as locks and river banks. Diving and swimming are not allowed in the waterways covered by this guide.

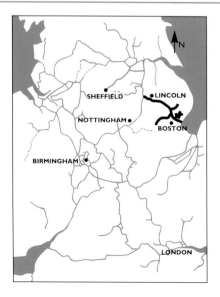

Wildlife

General Description

The mixed habitat along the disused railway, by the River Witham between Bardney and Boston, is a valuable wildlife corridor and a designated Nature Reserve. Its scrub/tree cover is essential to many bird species and greatly enhances the importance of the general corridor.

The lower Witham itself generally exhibits good water quality and supports a diverse range of fauna. In addition the various Delphs support some of the most interesting aquatic communities in the area. The Witham Navigable Drains have less wildlife, probably because of their more intensive management.

The full mixing of fish populations is prohibited by the sluices and locks which allow efficient drainage of the region.

Lincolnshire Trust for Nature Conservation.
(Telephone, see page 95).

Mute Swans

Birds

River Witham

Swallows, martins and swifts often swoop low over the bank tops, and barn owls use the old farm buildings as nest sites. Coots, moorhens, and mallards are widespread, together with sedge warblers, reed warblers, blackbirds, linnets and woodpigeons. Dogdyke Pumping Station is a good place to see heron, lapwings, greylag geese and pheasants.

The Delphs

These larger drains, especially Metheringham, support good bird groups including moorhen, heron, sedge warbler, reed warbler, teal, pochard, and shoveler.

Horncastle Canal/River Bain

The gravel-pit lakes near Kirkby-on-Bain have breeding groups of pochard, shelduck, little tern, and shoveler.

Near Coningsby Lock is a good breeding site for snipe. Little tern and tufted duck have also been recorded.

Moorhen

Plants

River Witham

The line of the old railway bankside downstream of Bardney has *scarlet pimpernel, common spotted-orchid, common twayblade, stonecrop, tufted vetch, false fox-sedge, hairy sedge* and *water dropwort*. The larger species include *hazel, alder, crab apple, blackthorn, ash* and *pedunculate oak*.

A detailed survey of the area just downstream of the Witham/Slea confluence found a total of 82 species. On the old railway these included *false oat, smooth hawksbeard, toadflax, goatsbeard, field horsetail* and *hop trefoil*.

River Slea/Kyme Eau

A similar river habitat to the majority of the area. A more valuable site is near Cobblers Lock where extensive reedbeds fringe the Slea and abundant *water violet* is present in the associated drains.

Horncastle Canal/River Bain

There is a reasonable diversity by Coningsby Lock, with *shining-* and *fennel-leaved pondweeds, creeping yellow cress, horned pondweed* and *hornwort*.

The Witham Navigable Drains

Fringed water-lily does well on the Maud Foster Drain.

The Delphs

The typical flora of Metheringham, Nocton, and Timberland Delphs includes *flowering rush, reed canary grass, yellow* and *white water-lilies, water dock, reed sweet-grass* and various sedges.

Common Mallow

Animals

There have been sightings of *otters* on the Metheringham Delph, and at the confluence of Barlings Eau and the Old River Witham (just downstream of Bardney lock).

Rabbits and *hares* generally abound in the area's open acres.

Insects

The Witham has a diverse range, including *water-boatmen* and *red-eyed damselflies*. *Meadow Brown* and *Ringlet* butterflies are found just downstream of the Witham/Slea confluence.

Fish

Recent surveys show that the River Witham and its tributaries support a Class A fishery. The area is a venue for major fishing matches, including National events.

The Witham itself is a well-balanced coarse fishery dominated by good numbers of *roach* with occasional high catches of large *common bream*. Also present are *silver bream*, *perch*, *pike*, *gudgeon* and *ruffe*. A similar mix is found in the Fossdyke.

Nocton and Timberland Delphs are well stocked with *common bream* and sometimes *silver bream*, with *roach* being generally less important. This is probably because bream are more suited to the sheltered habitats in these waterways.

There are high numbers of *roach* in the River Slea/Kyme Eau, with *rudd* and *bream* being significant on occasions at certain sites.

The Horncastle Canal and River Bain are mixed fisheries with *chub*, *dace* and *roach* dominant.

Peacock Butterfly

Navigational Information

The spine of the area is the River Witham, a wide, slow-flowing waterway, with the tide excluded and the levels controlled by the Grand Sluice at Boston. In times of low flow the Environment Agency augments the level in the Witham by pumping water from the Trent at Torksey, using the Fossdyke as a feeder. Access is from the River Trent at Torksey, and from the Wash at Boston. Although fairly large vessels can use the system, commercial traffic is rare with an occasional vessel using the Fossdyke/Witham route as a short cut to avoid the Humber. Most are deterred by Lincoln's restrictive High Bridge (Glory Hole).

Waterways

Fossdyke	11 miles
River Witham	32 miles
Sleaford Navigation.	Navigable for 7½ miles
Witham Drains.	A 40-mile navigable network
Horncastle Canal.	Un-navigable

Navigation Authorities

All telephone numbers are on page 94.
Fossdyke. British Waterways
River Witham (non-tidal). British Waterways
River Witham (tidal). Port of Boston

Navigable Drains:

Maud Foster, Stonebridge, West and East Fen Catchwaters. Unclear
Others. Witham Fourth District Internal Drainage Board.
Slea Navigation. None.

Maximum Dimensions (in feet)

Torksey Lock (Fossdyke) 170 x 16ft 6ins.
Stamp End Lock (Witham) 81 x 17
Bardney Lock (Witham) 81 x 17
Boston Grand Sluice Lock (Witham) 55 x 26
—but larger craft may pass (see page 87).
Bottom Lock (Slea) 72 x 14
Antons Gowt Lock (Drains) 81 x 16ft 9ins
Cowbridge Lock (Drains) 71 x 10ft 9ins (no more than 65ft for broad-beam craft).

The Glory Hole (High Bridge), Lincoln

This ancient and beautiful bridge is the most restricted part of the main Fossdyke/Witham through route. 15ft wide. Air draught and water depth obviously depend on river levels but in normal conditions the arch has an air draught of 7ft 6ins at the sides, and 9ft 6ins in the centre. Water depth is normally 3–4ft.

Locks.

Torksey and Boston locks are manned by BW staff and may be called on Marine Band radio, Channel 74.
All other locks are crew-operated.

Turning/winding

Longer craft on the Fossdyke cannot turn in the normal width of the canal, and a number of turning points are marked on the maps. The River Witham is wide enough for all craft to turn.

Speed Limits

Fossdyke, and Witham upstream of Stamp End Lock (Lincoln) 4mph.
The remainder of the Witham, 6mph.
Slea and Navigable Drains. 4mph

Facilities

As marked on the maps.
Moorings on the Witham downstream of Bardney are at floating pontoons.
Laundry. Lincoln (Brayford Pool), Dunston Fen, and Orchard Caravans (Chapel Hill).
Pump-outs. Torksey, and Lincoln
Petrol/Diesel. Lincoln, other sites on maps.
Showers. Torksey, Lincoln, Bardney.

Slipways

Brayford Pool, Lincoln (page 31); Kendall's Boatyard (Lincoln Marina); Hornblower's Pub (Belle Isle Marina, Dogdyke).

Head of Navigation Plaques

Plaques are available for reaching Cobblers Lock (Slea, page 70), and for passing through Cowbridge Lock (Drains, page 66).

Crossing the Wash.

It needs careful planning, especially by narrow-boaters. Changing channels in the Wash needs careful navigation by all craft. See page 87.

By-Waters

Are sometimes navigated, eg Timberland Delph, (map 7, pages 44-45) but such waterways are at the boater's own risk. Nevertheless they are a lure for those who like to visit every nook and cranny. Thought needs to be given to turning round, and water depths cannot be guaranteed.

Many side waterways have *'pointing doors'* at the entrance. These are gates which are only closed during floods to stop high levels in the Witham from entering. Leave them as you find them.

Water levels in this area are managed to suit all users but in an emergency navigation is always subservient to the vital needs of irrigation, drainage and flood defences.

'CLOSED SEASON' FOR MOORING, AND WINTER WATER LEVELS

From 1st November to 1st April the Environment Agency does not allow mooring on the River Witham between Boston and Chapel Hill *but passage of the river and locks is still allowed by BW*

During the same period the level of the river is reduced by approx 2ft at Boston Grand Sluice and therefore upstream to Bardney Lock at which the level is down by approx 1ft. This is to make more capacity in the river and the flood plain to allow for containment of winter rain and snowfall thereby preventing flooding of the low lying lands.

Also during this period—BW require 48hrs notice of passage of Boston Grand Sluice lock. The Slea is closed to navigation.

See pages 87 and 88 for navigational access details from the Trent and the Wash

13

The level Lincolnshire countryside is ideal for exploration by bike, many boaters carry them on board

Viking Way fingerpost

Other Users

Walking

Paths are marked on the maps. Downstream of Lincoln this includes the central section of *The Viking Way*. This is a long distance foot-path which goes from the Humber Bridge to Rutland Water near Oakham. It is waymarked with a Viking helmet symbol. The route passes near Washingborough, Bardney, Southrey, and Stixwould. Using an old railway track it also follows the Horncastle Canal for half of its route from its name town to Woodhall Spa. The route booklet (ISBN 0-86111-110-9) is available from Recreational Services, Lincolnshire County Council, County Offices, Lincoln LN1 1YL. (Telephone, see page 94).

Stepping Out Walks

There are twelve waymarked and interesting walks in this series. They include the rivers Witham and Slea, and the Roman Car Dyke. Leaflets from Sleaford Tourist Information. (Telephone, see page 95).

Havenside Country Park

In the early stages of development. It extends along the tidal section of the Witham, to the mud-flats of the Wash and the coastal path, past the Pilgrim Fathers Memorial, northwards to Skegness. The park uses the towpath and north bank of the Witham from the end of the Maud Foster drain, by the church.

Long distance walkers can follow the route from Torksey to Boston and the coast but will need to divert from the river bank onto the Viking Way between Bardney Bridge and Kirkstead Bridge. (See maps 5 and 6).

Cycling

British Waterways do not allow cycling on any part of the towpaths along the Fossdyke and the River Witham. However, Sustrans, a national charity promoting the development of cycle-ways, is planning to use the banks of the River Witham between Lincoln and Boston as part of Route 1 of the proposed National Cycle Network. This will be signed accordingly. It may be 1998 before this is finalised and it is not yet known which bank will be used for which stretch of the route.

Using a bicycle in conjunction with a boat holiday is an ideal way to explore the Lincolnshire countryside and the many tourist attractions near the waterways.

Helpful are cycle trails using the waterways as a base, such as the routes based on the Fossdyke, published by West Lindsey District Council in 1997. Available from Gainsborough Tourist Information, (see page 95).

Sleaford area

There are a number of linked rides along pleasant country lanes with little traffic. Described in a leaflet from Sleaford Tourist Information, (see page 95).

An informative Cycling in Lincolnshire leaflet is available from Lincolnshire Tourism, Lincoln Castle, Lincoln LN1 3AA.

Angling

The following rules apply to all anglers on non-tidal waters, including those fishing from a boat. It is an offence not to produce a valid licence while fishing when required to do so.

An annual National Rod Licence is needed by all anglers over the age of 12, obtainable from Post Offices. Short term licences are available for holiday use, as well as concessionary terms for those 12–16 years old, or over 65. *In addition* the permission of the holder of the fishing rights is necessary, usually by the purchase of a Day Ticket from a Bailiff on the bank.

The catchment is characterised by slow moving watercourses and seasonal fluctuations of river levels dictated by flood defence and agricultural requirements. Fish species are listed on page 11.

Angling Clubs

The holders of the fishing rights in this area are as follows: (Telephone, see page 95)

Witham & District Joint Angling Federation. An association of seven clubs, with the rights to much of the Witham, Timberland Delph, Billinghay Skirth, and part of the Horncastle Canal.

Lincoln & District Angling Association. River Till

Horncastle Angling Club A section of the Horncastle Canal

Boston Angling Association Sibsey Trader Drain

British Waterways The Fossdyke. This is a direct controlled waterway, and permits are sold daily by the BW bailiff on the bank.

Windmills

Many of the area's windmills were used to power the pumps which kept Lincolnshire's fenlands drained. Eventually replaced by steam, diesel, and electricity all of the pumping type have disappeared from the landscape. Those remaining are grinding mills, including Heckington, unique with its eight sails, Alford with five sails, and Burgh le Marsh with its unusual left-handed sails. Fourteen windmills are included in a leaflet from the county's Tourist Information Centres (see page 95).

Ellis', Sibsey Trader, and Maud Foster can be visited from the waterways in this guide.

Sibsey Trader Mill from Stonebridge Drain

Maud Foster Mill at Boston

Ellis' Mill, Lincoln

Money's Mill, Sleaford, is the town's tourist information office

A General History of Fenland Waterways

Throughout England the great rivers were used to distribute goods far inland. In fenland areas navigation was more widespread with the extensive network of drainage watercourses also functioning as a transport system. The Fossdyke was built by the Romans, perhaps primarily for drainage with navigation as an added benefit.

Over the centuries the pattern of the low-lying fens changed as more and more acres were drained. Which channels were used solely for drainage and which also for navigation is the subject of on-going research but the pattern continues today. Each winter, boats are banned from mooring on the lower reaches of the River Witham as its duel drainage and water-retention role takes precedence over other uses.

In the late middle ages the climate deteriorated and fenland sheep farming declined. The water channels were neglected and it was not until the mid-1600s that major works once again took place with the South Forty Foot navigable drain being built from Boston to Bourne.

Below Sea-level

The fens were originally low-lying marshes, frequently flooded by fresh water coming down from the higher areas further inland, and by the sea at high tides. Drainage and drying caused the peaty soil to contract and the land sank below sea-level. High banks were built along the rivers to keep them confined, the adjacent fields sinking lower with each passing century. Windmills became a common sight, working incessantly to pump water UP from the fields and into the rivers and drainage channels. From the 1820s steam-driven pumps took over, although less beautiful they were more reliable.

Within this specialised area the majority of fenland boat traffic supported local trade but with the onset of the Canal Age in the 1760s waterways such as the Fossdyke and the River Witham became conduits for inland cargoes to and from the Midlands and Yorkshire, and sea-borne trade via Hull and Boston.

Sheffield Size

Boats were now larger and more heavily laden. Yorkshire keels became the usual craft on the north Lincolnshire waterways, they varied in size according to the dimension of their home canal but the widely used 'Sheffield size' keels were 61 feet long and 15 feet wide. Such craft were the work-horses of inland waterway transport well into the 20th century. To cater for them locks on the Fossdyke and the River

Witham were enlarged and the new canals to Sleaford and Horncastle were built to bring keels and their cargoes to those towns.

Coastal Access

The Witham's route to The Wash also gave coastal access to inland boats, and a safe inland route for sea-going craft wishing to reach the Trent and other major rivers of the north-east. In the 18th and 19th centuries boatmen would take their vessels wherever a cargo could be found. This applied not only to the skippers of keels and sloops but also to the narrowboat men from the Chesterfield Canal, bringing coal not only to Lincoln and Boston but also to Spalding via The Wash.

One problem, worsened by the large craft arriving from other areas, was the constrictive size of the single span High Bridge in central Lincoln. The water depth below it was increased in 1795 but it has always impeded navigation. Medieval in origin and topped with Tudor buildings the High Bridge, or Glory Hole as it is also known, is now one of the 'wonders of the waterways'. Passing beneath it is a highlight for the crews of today's leisure craft but its single span still prevents large commercial vessels passing along the otherwise convenient Fossdyke/Witham route between the Trent and the coast.

Sir Joseph Banks

In the second half of the 18th century Lincolnshire was fortunate in having as a resident a man of national stature. Sir Joseph Banks, who lived near Horncastle, was a major influence in the construction of the waterways in the north of the county—the Slea Navigation, Horncastle Canal, the Grantham Canal and improvements to the River Witham.

Banks' fame was based on his voyage with Captain Cook to the South Seas, as expedition botanist, from which he returned in 1768. His scientific analysis of the information he brought back led him to the Presidency of the prestigious Royal Society, a baronetcy, and the friendship of the King.

He helped Lincolnshire waterway projects financially as well as using his towering reputation to influence parliamentary committees and to combat the objections of powerful special interest groups. His knowledge was boosted by his role as a commissioner on the local drainage boards, an appointment which gave him unparalleled knowledge of all aspects of fenland waterways.

The History of the
Fossdyke and River Witham

Lincolnshire is not entirely flat and the River Witham flows through a gap in the Lincoln ridge. Thousands of years ago lakes formed there, the largest of which is now called Brayford Pool. When the Romans arrived they found a natural site for a settlement. The soldiers set up a military station on the ridge, their engineers made the Witham navigable downstream to the coast, excavated Brayford Pool as an inland port and dug the Fossdyke.

The Fossdyke is claimed to be the oldest canal in Britain still in use, but whether the Romans created it for drainage or transport is still open to question. However, recent research indicates that it was a navigable link to the River Trent and part of a network of canals and rivers linking the Roman cities of Lincoln and York.

Danes and Normans

In later centuries the Danes invaded Lincolnshire by sailing along the Fossdyke, and the Normans used it to carry the stone for building Lincoln's cathedral and castle. Waterway maintenance in later centuries was inefficient but in the 13th century Lincoln was still England's fourth largest port.

Such was the importance to Lincoln of the Fossdyke and the River Witham that the City Corporation took over responsibility for the two waterways in 1670. The Fossdyke was leased to various parties over the centuries on the understanding that they would maintain the waterway from the trading profits they made. This arrangement had mixed results but in 1740 it was taken over by Richard Ellison of Thorne and conditions improved.

In the 1760s the lower reaches of the Witham were improved when the river levels were raised and the tide excluded by the completion of the Grand Sluice and its lock at Boston.

Cargoes

In such a low-lying county land drainage is paramount and major improvement schemes usually involved the Witham. In the 18th and 19th centuries this was the work of the nationally famous engineers: John Smeaton, William Jessop and John Rennie—pacifying the conflicting drainage and navigation lobbies needed men of status and wide experience. This was also the heyday of trade on the local waterways and in Brayford Pool the wharves were crowded with keels bringing corn, seed and grain to and from the adjacent warehouses, mills and breweries. A major trade also developed in wool to the West Riding of Yorkshire, as well as ale, and timber for pit-props. Coal was the major return cargo but the keels also brought in hardware, linen, cotton goods and earthenware from the industrialised areas.

High Bridge

Improvements were continually made to the Fossdyke and the Witham but one feature always caused navigational problems. Spanning the Witham in the centre of Lincoln is the High Bridge, also known as the Glory Hole. This is a medieval structure, topped by beautiful half-timbered Tudor buildings, which was too narrow and low for large boats.

In 1792 Lincoln Corporation asked William Jessop to suggest ways of solving the navigational problems caused by the single-span High Bridge. He suggested taking up the underwater wooden floor upon which the bridge was built and under-pinning the walls. This would give more depth of water for the laden boats. The Corporation agreed but nothing was done until 1795. A proportion of the cost was paid by the proprietors of the Slea Navigation and the Horncastle Canal, in the knowledge that profits would increase if larger boats could reach their new waterways via the Glory Hole.

The improvements increased trade throughout the area and more money was then available for other works on the Witham. In Boston the shipping trade from the coast was stagnating because of the mud in the tidal section of the river and this and other problems were alleviated by major schemes in the first decades of the 19th century. Between Lincoln and Boston the Witham was straightened and deepened and locks were realigned. Public passenger boats provided a cheap and popular service along the Witham and the river became the central strand of transport in the area.

In the 20th century traffic lessened. Regular barge traffic on the Witham ceased in 1952, although there was some timber cargo to Boston in the 1960s. Commercial carrying along the Fossdyke to Lincoln ceased in 1972.

In 1964 Brayford Pool was cleared, 25 wrecked boats were removed, then in 1969 the Brayford Trust was formed to watch over Lincoln's lake. Improvements for boaters and other visitors continue to this day and Brayford Pool has become a popular area of the city of Lincoln.

Map 1: *Fossdyke*
Torksey – Saxilby
2¹/₂ miles

General Area
The Fossdyke is Britain's oldest canal still in use. Built by the Romans it linked Lindum (Lincoln) to the Trent, perhaps as part of a route to Eboracum (York).

Between Torksey lock and Saxilby the canal is quiet and remote between grassed flood banks. Then the A57 comes alongside, though it is not the busiest of trunk routes.

Torksey Lock
Above the lock. A sheltered and controlled area where activity depends on the Trent tide times, especially on summer weekends when boats jostle to go through the lock. When the tide is unsuitable everything is very quiet.

It is a colourful scene with the lock decorated with flowers in baskets, beds, and boxes. The Wheelhouse Restaurant also has a tidy, colourful garden behind wrought iron fencing. The grassy path along the top of flood bank can be walked towards Lincoln—a quiet stroll, with bird calls, moored boats, and whispering fields.

Below the lock. The impact of the Trent is obvious. The path down to the river is across the road and through a white gate, (sheep graze here so dogs must be kept on a lead). It seems more remote than it actually is, a perpetual breeze blows, and the river smells damp. Normal flow is left to right, if the Trent is going right to left the tide is coming in.

Torksey Village
A noisy walk along the main road, close by the castle. The Hume Arms is a pleasant pub/restaurant.

Torksey Castle
The name is misleading because it has never been a castle. Built as a house in 1560 it probably got its name after a skirmish in the Civil War. It was the base for a garrison of Parliamentary troops until they were routed in 1645 by two hundred Royalists. The house was set on fire, never rebuilt, and plundered for building materials. It has stood as a ruin for over 360 years. No public access.

Saxilby
A large village but a by-pass keeps the A57 traffic away. The willow-draped grassy bank is often lined with visiting boats and opposite a floodwall protects the adjacent road.

There used to be a swing-bridge here, and the semi-circular recess of its pivot can be seen in the stonework under the footbridge, together with information panels. Opened to allow the sailing keels to pass, it was always a bottleneck and was demolished in 1937.

The footbridge was installed in 1987 when it was already 103 years old. It originally spanned the main line of the Great Northern Railway at Newark but it was moved to Saxilby to give access to the pleasant walks and moorings on the far bank.

Navigation
Torksey
The lock-cut from the Trent is a safe haven, with *floating mooring-pontoons* allowing for the Trent's tidal rise and fall. *Traffic lights* control entry to the lock which is operated by the keeper, see page 88. The lock is a listed structure and the gates are opened and closed by turning *capstans* on the lockside. Book in with the keeper at busy times. When locking out into the Trent, for safety reasons, tell keeper *your destination* so that arrival can be checked. (Telephone, see page 94).

The lock has flood gates allowing usage when the water level in the Trent is higher than that in the Fossdyke. In 1997, the lock chamber was lengthened as part of the areas flood defences. The bottom gates are mechanised and the *new dimensions* are on page 12.

Moorings. Short-term, by the lock for use of the facilities only. Visitor (72hr), beyond the permanent moorings. At the lockside road exit there is a noticeboard with visitor information and a local map.

Saxilby
72hr visitor moorings, with grassy banks, picnic tables, barbecue sites, and willow trees.

The water point is at the 1hr moorings by the road, the rubbish disposal is by the footbridge, and the elsan toilet disposal facility is in the Gents across the road.

Also near the footbridge is a map of shop locations, a little out of date, but the canalside Wayward Sole has visitor information (and good fish & chips). There is a hairdressers, and Tong's DIY shop-cum-engineering works, useful for many items including Calor gas, open every day but not Sunday pm. Also a general grocery store, phone box, Post Office, all 300 yards into village. Pharmacy at the Co-op supermarket, ¹/₂ mile.

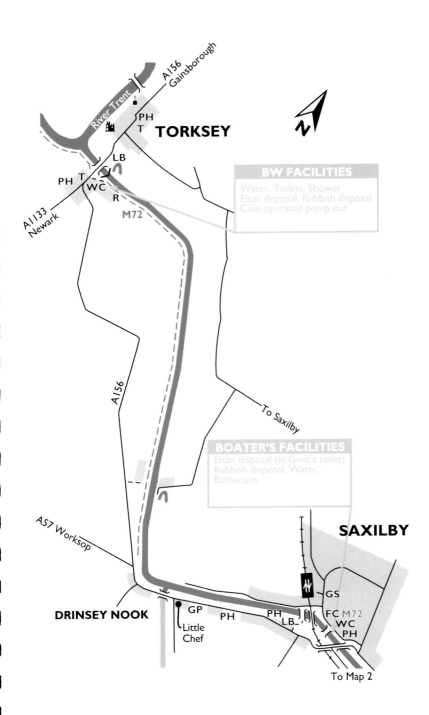

A156
Gainsborough

River Trent

PH
T
TORKSEY

LB
PH T
WC
R
M72

A1133
Newark

A156

To Saxilby

SAXILBY

A57 Worksop

GS

DRINSEY NOOK
GP
PH
Little
Chef
PH
LB
FC M72
WC
PH

To Map 2

Torksey Lock

Torksey Lock gates are operated by capstans

Visitor moorings, Saxilby

Map 2: *Fossdyke*
Saxilby – Lincoln West
4¹/₂ miles

General Area

Although the whole of this section is now known as the Fossdyke, the true Roman canal is only the length between Torksey and Odder. The remainder of the route between Odder and Lincoln is really the straightened course of the River Till. This distinction is more noticeable near Lincoln where the waterway looks less artificial.

The A57 crossing and the railway are minor disturbances to the general peace and quiet. The surrounding land was drained in 1804 as part of John Rennie's improvements to the River Witham.

To the east, Lincoln scarp, a ridge of limestone running through to the Cotswolds, proves there are hills in this generally flat county. On its heights the distinctive towers of Lincoln cathedral can be seen, clearly outlined on the skyline.

Sailing Keels

The Fossdyke's working boats were the keels which sailed many of the routes in this part of England.

A typical example in the 1930s was the *Excelsior*. She loaded 18-stone sacks of wheat from silos in Hull's King George dock, then took the cargo up the Humber, along the Trent to Torksey, and along the Fossdyke to the north side of Lincoln's Brayford Pool, from where horse-drawn drays took it to Henry Le Tall's mill. Such a trip could take as long as two weeks. Timber was also carried to Saxilby, and bulk wheat to Lincoln's Hovis mill.

Steam-tugs operated on the Humber and Trent and the keels could often make swift progress by being towed all the way between Hull and Torksey. They then had to use their sails on the Fossdyke, and sometimes this section of the journey would take longer than the much longer passage from Hull docks. Sometimes, if there was no fair wind, the wife and son of the *Excelsior's* master would, with a rope and harnesses, pull the keel along the Fossdyke, the lad always remembering his mother saying *'Come on Jess. Dig your toes in and pull.'*

There were small steam-tugs for hire on the Fossdyke but they were notoriously under-powered and most keelmen considered them to be more of a hindrance than a help.

On the wide waters of the Humber and Trent, keels could carry 100–120 tons, but on the restricted Fossdyke the maximum was only 80–90 tons. When leaving the Trent this problem was solved by unloading part of a keel's cargo into a lighter which was kept at Torksey for the purpose. This was then towed behind the keel on the trip to Lincoln.

Odder

Here the River Till merges with the Fossdyke, its levels and flow quite substantial between its reed-lined banks in rainy periods.

Fertiliser Factory

The former fertiliser factory, on the waterside just outside Saxilby, is now a timber store and a park for light industries such as joinery and furniture making.

In its previous role the factory, established in 1863, used the Fossdyke for transport, as well as road and rail. In its early days bone knife-handle waste was brought here from Sheffield by boat. Use of the factory's wharf continued up to c1970.

The Pyewipe Inn

This pub's odd name is a local term for the peewit, a common bird in this area.

Lincolnshire Narrowboat Trust

If you see *The Brayford King* you may wonder why a boat 12ft wide belongs to The Lincolnshire Narrowboat Trust. The organisation was founded in 1990 when it was assumed that a narrowboat would be converted to provide holidays for disabled people. However, further planning proved that a wide-beam boat would be more suitable and the final result was a 63ft × 12ft Dutch barge-style craft. It is fully equipped for the needs of the disabled, including a wheelchair lift, and can take up to eleven people on day, evening, weekend, or week-long trips on the Fossdyke and Witham. (Telephone, see page 94).

Navigation
The Woodcocks

Pub, restaurant, ideal facilities for families with small children, play area, grass and wooded surroundings, good moorings at grassy bank. A planning application for a marina is being discussed.

Pyewipe Inn

Moorings at pub.

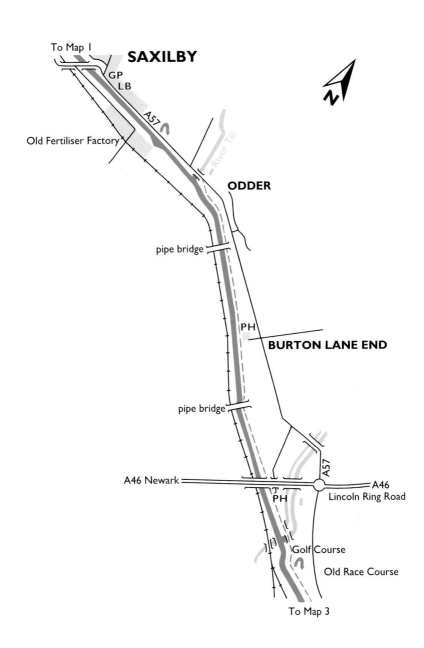

SAXILBY

To Map 1

GP
LB

A57

Old Fertiliser Factory

River Till

ODDER

pipe bridge

PH

BURTON LANE END

pipe bridge

A57

A46 Newark

A46
Lincoln Ring Road

PH

Golf Course

Old Race Course

To Map 3

Lincoln

Lincoln is not only an historic city but also a busy pedestrianised shopping centre, with a popular indoor market. The waterfront has always been an important feature of Lincoln's history but now it is being revitalised for the future.

In recent times the 'up the hill' tourist attractions of the cathedral and castle have drawn attention away from the lower areas of the city now that Brayford Pool is no longer busy with working boats. However the old waters now have a new focus, the south bank lined with the buildings of the University of Lincolnshire, officially opened by HM the Queen in October 1996.

Further features are the new high-level road bridge at the Pool's western entrance (spring 1997), and developments at Lincoln Marina. (1997).

Plans are also in hand to hold an annual 'Mayor's Regatta' event in Brayford Pool as a celebration of Lincoln's waterways.

This new focus on the city's waterfront is a reflection of the area's past prominence. In Viking times Brayford Pool was a thriving port receiving goods from Scandinavia and Europe. Later the Normans landed stone for building their cathedral and castle, and in the medieval era the port made Lincoln a main centre for the wool trade. The busiest years were probably in the 18th and 19th centuries when the wharves bustled with keels bringing grain, seed, and other products to the mills, warehouses, and breweries lining the Pool's banks.

'Up Hill Lincoln'

A second gate to the castle has now been opened and the cathedral, castle, and The Lawn area now form an easily visited 'chain' of sites on the hill.

The easiest way to visit the city's many attractions, without puffing your way uphill, is to use the *Sightseeing Bus.*

This is an open-top double-decker, which goes from a bus-stop on the northern side of Brayford Pool, near the visitor moorings. Tickets for sale on the bus, valid all day, get on and off as many times as you like, or stay on for a one hour ride with commentary by a local Blue-Badge Guide. Daily, every 30 mins, May–Sep; weekends Easter—end Oct. Adults £4, children £1.50, family ticket £10. (Telephone, see page 95).

Lincoln Cathedral. One of the finest medieval buildings in Europe. High on its hill, overlooking the ancient city and dominating the skyline for many miles. Inside the glorious colour from the windows plays on the soaring pillars of local limestone and Purbeck marble.

There is also The Airmen's Chapel containing memorial books of aircrew killed in action flying from Lincolnshire's many RAF bases, see page 47.

Lincoln Castle. This ancient fortress is situated next to the cathedral, once guarding the busy markets of the city and wharves of the River Witham. On the western side of the hill it looks towards the Trent which more than once proved a convenient highway for invaders.

The walls can be walked, and from the top of Observatory Tower the River Witham can be seen stretching towards the east, its course marked by the cylindrical vats of the sugar factory at Bardney, and in the far distance the famous 'Stump' of Boston's church. To the west the River Trent is marked by the cooling towers of three of the power stations which use its water, dwarfed by distance.

There is also a rare chance to see the *Magna Carta,* one of only four in existence. A well designed exhibition tells the story of this document's place in the democratic history of the world, leading through to an inner sanctum where the Magna Carta is kept in a temperature- and light-controlled environment.

Castle open all year, Mon–Sat 09.30–17.30, Sun 11.00–17.30. Winter closing 16.00. Guided tours 11.00 and 14.00. Tickets are valid all day. (Telephone, see page 95).

Incredibly Fantastic Old Toy Show. 26 Westgate, Lincoln. Easter Sat–end Sep, Tues to Sat, 11.00–17.00, Sun 12.00–16.00. (Telephone, see page 95).

The Lawn. Impressive Georgian building in nine acres, with picnic tables, pub/restaurant, small arcade specialist shops. Sir Joseph Banks' Conservatory is a 5,000 sq ft tropical glasshouse containing exotic plant species found by the Lincolnshire explorer who accompanied Captain Cook to Australia. Also an aquarium .

Near the cathedral and castle. Admission free. Open daily, summer 09.30–17.00, winter 10.30–16.00. (Telephone, see page 95).

Usher Art Gallery. Many fine works of art including past scenes of Brayford Pool. Also porcelain, silver, clocks, watches, coins. Open Mon–Sat 10.00—17.30. Sun 14.30–17.00. Closed Good Friday, 25–26 Dec and 1 Jan. (Telephone, see page 95).

Ellis' Mill. High on the hill. Flour for sale, wind willing. The tower was built in 1798 and it worked until the 1940s. After that it became derelict until it was restored by the Lincoln Civic Trust and ground its first flour for 40 years in April 1981. Open, May–Sep, Sat & Sun, 14.00–18.00. Oct–Apr, 2nd and 4th weekends, 14.00–dusk. (Telephone, see page 95).

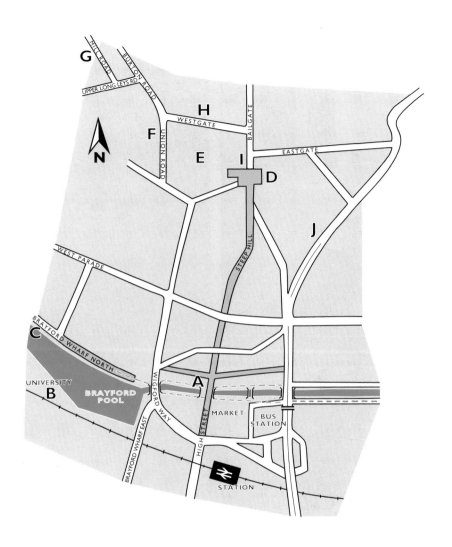

Key:

| Pedestrian area |

- **A** High Bridge/Glory Hole
- **B** University
- **C** Sightseeing bus stop
- **D** Cathedral
- **E** Castle
- **F** The Lawn
- **G** Ellis' Mill
- **H** Incredibly Fantastic Old Toy Show
- **I** Tourist Information
- **J** Usher Art Gallery

Lincoln

Glory Hole

Steep Hill

Brayford Pool and the Cathedral

The University

Map 3: *Fossdyke/River Witham*
Lincoln West – Washingborough
3 $\frac{1}{2}$ miles

General Area
A beautiful and absorbing passage through an ancient city.

The approach from the west is marked by moored boats all along the south bank—a wide variety of craft, some unusual, of all sizes, on long-term and residential moorings.

There are classic views of the cathedral from Brayford Pool. Many artists have painted the scene over the centuries and examples can be seen in the Usher Art Gallery. They show activity in the Pool has changed considerably, but the cathedral overlooking it is timeless.

An unmissable fact is that Lincoln has swans like other places have ducks.

A highlight is passing under the Glory Hole, one of England's most historic bridges.

Downstream of Stamp End Lock the waterway goes through a short industrial area, before returning to the open countryside.

Brayford Pool
The Pool is a quiet haven in busy Lincoln, ringed with moored craft, a floating restaurant, and overlooked by a wide variety of buildings. Local people eat lunchtime sandwiches on its banks, and tourists wander along the short stretch between the Pool and the Glory Hole.

The south bank has undergone major changes with the construction of the waterside University of Lincolnshire, which, in turn, is acting as a magnet for further improvements.

The trip boat *City of Lincoln* operates from outside the Royal William IV pub. (Telephone, see page 94).

Glory Hole (High Bridge)
This is the oldest bridge in this country with buildings still upon it. The barrel-vaulted span is Norman. It had shops on it in the 14th century, but it was widened in 1540 when the half-timbered buildings now seen were erected. It was refurbished in the 1920s.

Navigation
The BW facilities are adjacent to the Section Inspector's office.

Brayford Pool.
Harbourmaster's Office. Visitor moorings at jetties: day mooring £2; per night £3.50; seven nights (paid in advance) £19. (Telephone, see page 94).

The toilets, showers, and laundry need a code number to unlock them; changed regularly these are available from the Harbourmaster or local boaters. The fees for the coin-operated laundry are: washer £1; dryer 50p. Moor in front of the building only for the water-points, pump-out, and rubbish disposal. The pump-out (£4) is operated by the Harbourmaster who is usually in attendance throughout the mornings, daily.

Slipway in south-east corner, suitable for craft up to 18ft, no charge.

Lincoln Marina. Breakdown repairs. (Telephone, see page 94).

Shopping. All city-centre facilities within a short walk of the visitor moorings.

The Pool's eastern exit is narrow and not easy to see on a first visit. Aim for the building clearly marked 'Marks & Spencer', as you approach it you will see the narrow exit, and usually trip boats, masses of swans, and sightseers.

Glory Hole (High Bridge)
Restricted air draught and width (see page 12). No towpath through. Good, free moorings for shopping downstream, near the Witch & Wardrobe pub, (see front cover), but probably too lively for an overnight stop. There are gates through the railings, need BW Watermate key.

Stamp End Lock
Guillotine top gate, powered, crew operated, BW Watermate key needed. Follow the instructions on the control box. The key can only be withdrawn when everything has been done as instructed and the top gate is fully descended. Moorings above and below for lock crew.

Walking
There is no towpath under the Glory Hole. Steps alongside it give access to the busy but pleasant pedestrianised High Street. Straight across, and down to the towpath again.

The dual-carriageway road bridge has no towpath. Use the north bank, via pelican crossing, or better via south bank and footbridge over the road. Walk on the south bank to Stamp End Lock.

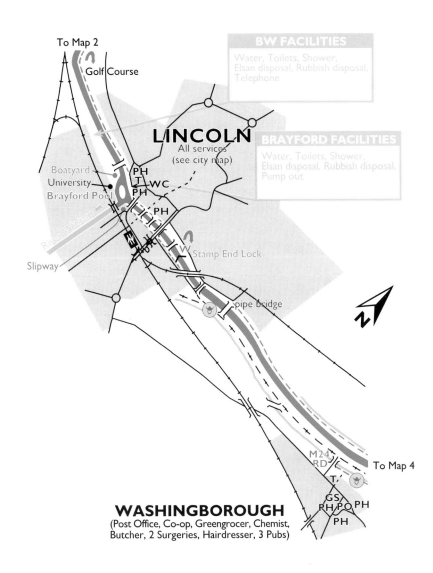

To Map 2

Golf Course

LINCOLN
All services
(see city map)

To Map 2

Boatyard
University
Brayford Pool

PH
T
PH
WC

PH

Slipway

W Stamp End Lock

pipe bridge

To Map 4

M24
RD

T

GS
PH PO PH

PH

WASHINGBOROUGH
(Post Office, Co-op, Greengrocer, Chemist,
Butcher, 2 Surgeries, Hairdresser, 3 Pubs)

BW FACILITIES
Water, Toilets, Shower,
Elsan disposal, Rubbish disposal,
Telephone

BRAYFORD FACILITIES
Water, Toilets, Shower,
Elsan disposal, Rubbish disposal,
Pump out

31

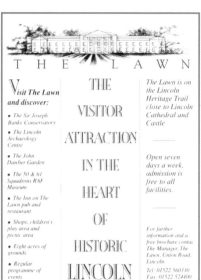

Lincoln—Glory Hole

Moorings near the Witch & Wardrobe are ideal for the shopping centre and market

Washingborough church

The town sign depicts the river ferry

Tyrwhitt Arms, Short Ferry

Map 4: *River Witham*
Washingborough – Bardney Lock
6 miles

General Area

A man-made section of the River Witham, hence its straightness. The floodbanks are low giving good views. Two other parallel water-courses accompany the river and as a result roads and buildings are kept some distance away. The scrubby washlands merge into arable areas, dotted with bushes and a few tall trees.

Below Bardney Lock a loop of the river's old course flows back in. Upstream, Lincoln cathedral can be seen outlined against the skyline.

Washingborough

A large village, on a ridge overlooking the river. The area near the Early English-style church is pleasant and the small ferry by which villagers used to cross the river is remembered in the name of the Ferryboat Inn. This is also the theme of Washingborough's village sign which was the first fruit of North Kesteven District Council's *Village Gateway* scheme, encouraging the creation of unique village location signs.

At the pontoon moorings the house is an old railway station.

The Car Dyke

An ancient water-course, running 76 miles from the River Witham, just west of Five Mile House, to the River Cam at Waterbeach in Cambridgeshire. It was thought to be a Roman Canal but in the 1970s a dedicated research group concluded that it was a catchwater drain which cleverly allowed water to flow in both directions depending on the state of the tide. It was also thought that the Romans used the fens for agriculture, but again recent research points to industrial activity, particularly the production of salt, deposited by high tides flowing over the low lands.

Five Mile House

Deriving its name from the distance from Lincoln this was once the site of an ex-boatman's inn although there are no buildings now.

The light-green footbridge was built in 1957, and replaced a chain-ferry. During dredging work a Saxon sword was found, and in surrounding villages more than a dozen prehistoric 'dug-out' boats hewn from single trees have been found.

In October 1848 the Great Northern Railway was built between Lincoln and Boston, here using the south bank of the Witham. There was a station here for Fiskerton, with the ferry crossing to the village. The station closed in 1958. The last passenger train ran on the line in October 1970, and the last goods train in 1981.

Short Ferry

This is the current limit of navigation on the old river Witham and its tributary the Barlings Eau. The road crossing near the Tyrwhitt Arms pub was a toll bridge until 1938.

Navigation
Washingborough

24hr pontoon moorings, rubbish disposal. Helpful information boards at the moorings have a village map, a short history, and the location of shops, services, eats, etc.

It is only a short walk to the centre of the village.

Bardney Lock

There is a sharp turn into the lock when going upstream.

Manual operation, fixed windlasses, moorings for lock crew above and below. Moorings have the best TV reception possible, with the transmitter in sight to the north-east.

Old River Witham

Navigable, and the Barlings Eau, to the Tyrwhitt Arms. Branch off below Bardney Lock, and after the bailey-bridge turn right. Craft up to 50ft can turn at the Tyrwhitt Arms, longer will need to reverse to the junction with the Old River Witham. Moorings are against a grassy bank.

Walking/Cycling

The Viking Way runs along the south bank of the South Delph the full length of this map. See page 15.

Leaflets for cycle routes in the Bardney area are available from Gainsborough Tourist Information. (Telephone, see page 95).

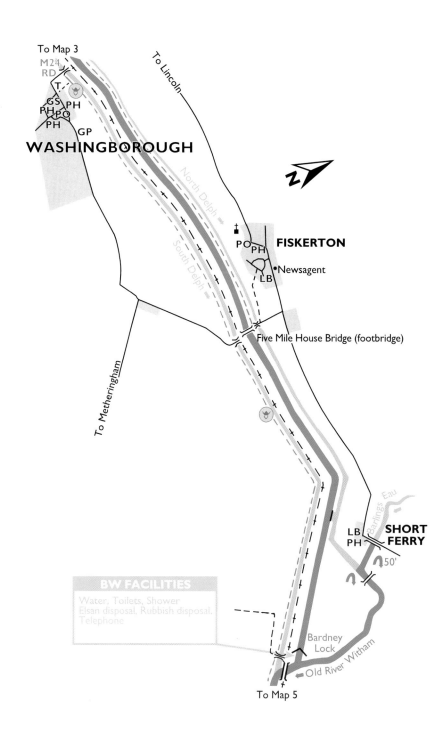

To Map 3

M24 RD

To Lincoln

T.

GS
PH
PH
PO

PH

GP

WASHINGBOROUGH

North Delph

South Delph

PO
PH   **FISKERTON**

•Newsagent

LB

Five Mile House Bridge (footbridge)

To Metheringham

Barlings Eau

LB
PH   **SHORT
FERRY**

50'

Bardney
Lock

Old River Witham

To Map 5

Bardney Lock

RAF memorial, Bardney Village Green

Visitor moorings, Dunston Fen, with Southrey beyond

37

Map 5: *River Witham*
Bardney Lock – Southrey
4 miles

General Area

The fringe of the Lincolnshire prairies; vast arable acres which produce a high percentage of England's crops. The only mature trees are usually around settlements, the houses and farms which dot the plains.

A typical East Anglian landmark is British Sugar's factory at Bardney which processes the sugar beet from the surrounding fields. Such works are noticeable for many miles and is certainly true of the tall cylindrical storage vats at Bardney.

The route of the dismantled Great Northern Railway follows the north bank between Bardney and Boston and some of the station buildings remain here and at many other locations along the river, usually converted to a modern use.

Bardney

A quiet village, the tower of its parish church visible from the river.

In Lincolnshire it is still asked of those who do not close a door *'do you come from Bardney?'* The reason is said to be because of an event at the great Benedictine Monastery which stood about one mile away. It is a local legend that in the year 675 those bearing the remains of the sainted King Oswald of Northumberland were refused admittance. During the night a great storm arose and an electrical force flung open the Abbey doors. This was deemed to be divine intervention so the King's remains were allowed in and the Abbey's doors were famously never closed again.

In the parish church there is a model of the Monastery at the time of its past glories.

On the village green, by the cross, a three-bladed propeller forms a floodlit RAF memorial to IX Squadron.

The old flat-bed ferry was replaced by the girder road bridge in about 1916.

Southrey

A small village and quiet rural backwater at the end of a lane that goes to the river and no further. However, the signs painted on the roof of the Riverside Inn are an obvious clue that there are less peaceful interludes.

When it was built in 1896 the pub's original owners would not have understood why it would be thought necessary to direct the following up to the sky—*If you can read this you'r to bloody close*, and to reinforce the message to the RAF pilots, *A.10s—Phantoms—Bulldogs—MOTs while you wait.*

The old railway station house remains, complete with platforms and name signs. The eaves are perfect for nests and in the summer swallows and martins swoop continuously around the old house.

Before the railway station opened the villagers used the Witham's popular packet-boat service to travel between Lincoln and Boston.

Navigation
Reduced Water Levels in Winter, and Mooring Prohibitions.

1st November to 1st April, see note, page 13.

Bardney

Pontoon moorings, 24hrs. Pubs and petrol nearby, half a mile to newsagents, Post Office, pharmacy and supermarket.

Southrey

No moorings to visit the village. It may be possible to tie-up to the ex-pontoon uprights but it would be difficult to get onto the bank. Beware slipway obstruction.

Dunston Fen

Good pontoon moorings, paid for by the White Horse pub so usage is £5, free if using the pub or taking a meal. Has a small caravan park and for a nominal fee boaters are welcome to use the showers, laundry and dryers.

Walking/Cycling
Viking Way

On the south bank from Bardney Lock to Bardney Bridge. No public path between Bardney and Dunston Fen.

Bardney will be near Route 1 of the proposed National Cycle Network, which will be signed accordingly. It may be 1998 before this is finalised. Leaflets for other cycle routes in the area are available from Gainsborough Tourist Information, (Telephone, see page 95).

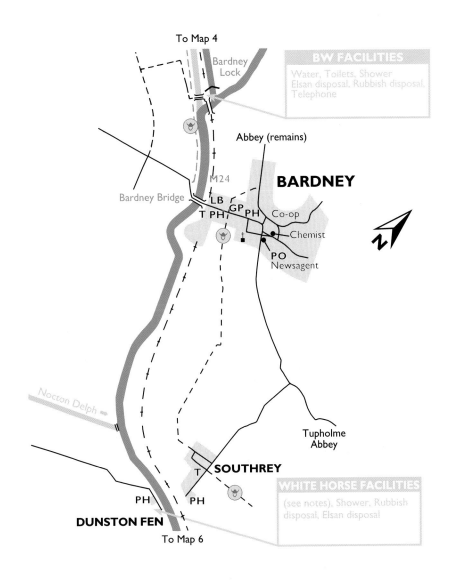

To Map 4

Bardney
Lock

Abbey (remains)

M24

BARDNEY

Bardney Bridge

LB
T PH
GP PH
Co-op

Chemist

PO
Newsagent

Nocton Delph

Tupholme
Abbey

T **SOUTHREY**

PH
PH

DUNSTON FEN

To Map 6

Map 6: *River Witham*
Southrey – Kirkstead Bridge
3½ miles

General Area

Quiet farmland, with scattered villages. To the south and west the drained fens are vast, remote and fertile. Depending on the season and weather they exude arable smells—damp earth, dry straw, mown grass. In the summer the plaintiff cry of the yellowhammer is often heard.

To the north and east the land rises slightly, eventually leading to the wooded oasis of Woodhall Spa.

Stixwould

One of the most noticeable landmarks along the River Witham is Stixwould's old railway signal-box, now converted to a house but retaining the style which clearly shows its original use. Adjacent to it are old platforms and level-crossing gates.

The village itself, over a mile from the river, had a Cistercian house of considerable wealth and much of the stone used to build the attractive parish church in the 1830s was said to be from the Abbey.

Kirkstead Bridge

Pontoon moorings for visiting Woodhall Spa, and with convenient pubs nearby. On the riverbank the owner of the old station has many lovingly restored relics of the railway.

Woodhall Spa

It is one mile to the centre of Woodhall Spa, a pleasant walk along a road lined with mature trees which meet to form a cover overhead. To the right, the gaunt remains of Kirkstead Abbey can be seen across the fields.

Woodhall Spa is a well kept town, with a peaceful village atmosphere, genteel hotels, fine-art shops, a speciality shop, and reminders of spa hey-days. Visitors still tend to promenade along.

The small town owes its existence to the accidental discovery of natural mineral water in the early 19th century. The search for coal was hindered by the water which kept entering the shaft, so much so that the works were abandoned in 1823. Eventually the problem water overflowed from the old pit into a ditch. The Lord of the Manor found the water beneficial for his gout, so he had it analysed and found it contained large quantities of sodium, calcium, and more bromine and iodine than the German spas then fashionable. So he built a pump-room and bath-house. This became fashionable in the 1850s when the new railways made travelling easy. Woodhall Spa's peak popularity was prior to WWI, the visitors valuing not only the water but also the fresh country air and the wooded seclusion.

Today the woods remain a striking feature—the pale blossom shades of spring, the rhododendrons in summer, and the russets and golds of autumn. They are also the location of the *Teahouse in the Woods*, built in 1907, and the *Kinema in the Woods*, still in use and called *'the flicks in the sticks'* by WWII RAF crews from nearby airfields.

Petwood House Hotel. A lovely building in extensive gardens. In World War II it was the Officers' Mess for 617 Squadron, (the Dambusters), now the Squadron Bar has an extensive display of war-time memorabilia, and is almost a shrine. The hotel is still entitled to fly the RAF ensign and proudly does so.

The RAF connection is most noticeably displayed by the *Dambusters' Memorial* in Royal Square. This commemorates the men of 617 Squadron who died on operations in 1943–45, and includes names from Canada, Australia and New Zealand.

Jubilee Park has a heated outdoor swimming pool, gardens, cafe, tennis, bowls, putting green, children's play area, and cycle hire.

Navigation

Reduced Water Levels in Winter, and Mooring Prohibitions.

1st November to 1st April, see note, page 13.

Kirkstead Bridge/ Woodhall Spa

24hr pontoon moorings at bridge. The best exit to the road is along the top of the bank, under the bridge, to the old railway station and platforms which were the junction for the Woodhall Spa branch line. Access to the road is just before. A few yards along the road is the Railway Hotel pub, a filling-station, telephone, and Post Office.

Walking

There is no public footpath between Dunston Fen and Kirkstead Bridge. The Viking Way can be followed, see page 15.

Woodhall Spa. There are many woodland walks based on the village, and bikes for hire.

Route leaflets are available from the Tourist Information Centre. (Telephone, see page 95).

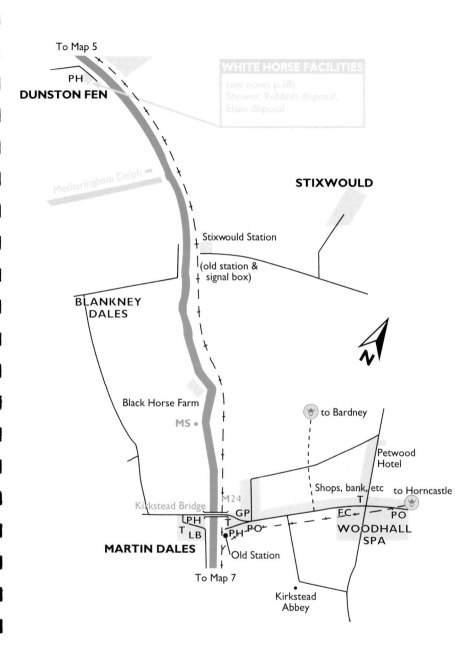

To Map 5

PH

DUNSTON FEN

Metheringham Delph

STIXWOULD

Stixwould Station

(old station &
signal box)

**BLANKNEY
DALES**

Black Horse Farm

MS •

to Bardney

Petwood
Hotel

Shops, bank, etc   to Horncastle

M24

Kirkstead Bridge   GP

PH   T   EC   PO

T   PH PO   **WOODHALL
LB   SPA**

MARTIN DALES   Old Station

To Map 7

Kirkstead
Abbey

41

Stixwould Station

The Petwood House Hotel, Woodhall Spa. The RAF ensign flying in memory of its use as the Officers' Mess of the Dambusters Squadron

WOODHALL SPA

Kirkstead Bridge visitor moorings

Map 7: *River Witham*
Kirkstead – Tattershall Bridge

4 miles

General Area

Quiet, apart from when aircraft are overhead, flying to or from their base at nearby RAF Coningsby. Think positively, it is an opportunity to see NATO strike fighters and AWACs (electronic reconnaissance aircraft)! And, the RAF is usually grounded at weekends.

Apart from these disturbances the area is quiet and unwinding. There is a lane along one bank but the traffic is infrequent, the houses along its route only showing as red-pantiled roofs from the river. Wild flowers are abundant, swallows twitter on the telephone wires, and swifts swoop low. Sometimes the drone of a distant tractor can be heard.

Timberland Pumping Station

Open to the public on the edge of a large area of fen. It is a place of great quiet and of wonderful open spaces.

The pumping station was built in 1839 to drain 2,500 acres of fenland. In 1976 it was replaced by a new electrically powered installation, still vital today for keeping the fen areas clear of water. There are special working open days.

An exhibition, *Tales of the River Bank*, explains how the fen was formed and how it is drained and used today. Open May–Oct, Wed–Sun 14.00–17.00. Nov–Apr, Sat–Sun, 13.00–16.00. Admission: Free. (See ad. page 72.)

Gibson's Cut

One and a half miles upstream of Tattershall Bridge there is a dip in the off-side flood bank. This is the closed entrance to Gibson's Cut and the remains of the short canal can be seen from the towpath. It was built to link Tattershall to the river, and was later superseded by the Horncastle Canal. (See page 78).

Navigation

Reduced Water Levels in Winter, and Mooring Prohibitions.
1st November to 1st April, see note, page 13.

Timberland Delph.
Sometimes visited by narrowboats and small craft. There are pointing doors at the entrance. It ends at the Roman waterway, the Car Dyke. There is no winding hole so boats must be able to turn in the width of the delph.

Walking/Cycling

A quiet lane runs along the flood bank from Kirkstead Bridge to Chapel Hill (map 8).

Timberland Delph

44

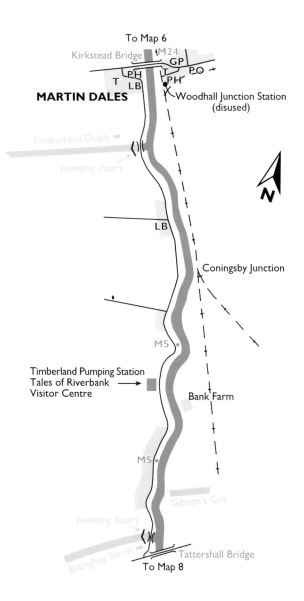

To Map 6

Kirkstead Bridge
M24
GP
PH
P.O
T
PH
T
LB

MARTIN DALES

Woodhall Junction Station
(disused)

Timberland Delph

pointing doors

LB

Coningsby Junction

N

MS

Timberland Pumping Station
Tales of Riverbank →
Visitor Centre

Bank Farm

MS

Gibson's Cut

pointing doors

Billinghay Skirth
Tattershall Bridge

To Map 8

Lancaster Bomber, "City of Lincoln"   © *Steve Barker BFN*
                                    (Courtesy The Battle of Britain Memorial Flight)

Dambusters Memorial, Woodhall Spa

Lincolnshire—Home of the Royal Air Force

Lincolnshire is justly proud of its links with military flying which go back to the early days of the Royal Flying Corps in World War I. The flimsy early aircraft flew from airfields on the edge of the Lincoln Ridge because they needed the updraught of air found there to get airborne.

The county's first aerodrome opened in July 1914 at Killingholme and by the end of 1918 Lincolnshire had 37 military airfields. In the usual way of things all but three closed after the Great War was won. In the 1930s the threat of war meant the RAF expanded again. By the time war was declared in 1939 ten new airfields were in active service with Handley Page Hampdens flying the first mission from RAF Waddington. Ideally placed for missions into Europe, by the end of 1945 there were 49 airfields in Lincolnshire, 28 of them bomber bases, more than in any other British county.

At the end of the World War II the capacity was again reduced.

Memorials

Reminders of the RAF and men of allied air-forces are all over the county—church windows, village memorials, parish halls, and in Lincoln Cathedral.

Along the River Witham there are memorials to IX Squadron at *Bardney* (see page 38), and to 617 Squadron, the Dambusters, at *Woodhall Spa* (page 40).

In *Lincoln Cathedral* the Airmen's Chapel contains memorial books with the names of 25,611 personnel who were killed in action flying from airfields in or near Lincolnshire the during WWII. The four stained glass windows in the Chapel are memorials to Bomber Command, the Royal Rhodesian Air Force, Flying Training Command, and the Royal New Zealand Air Force.

The Battle of Britain Memorial Flight.
(Map 8, page 49)

The Flight was formed in 1957 as a living tribute to all RAF air and ground crew who gave their lives in the second world war. It has been at RAF Coningsby since 1976 where aircraft bearing the most famous names in aviation history can be seen.

The Lancaster bomber proudly bears the name *City of Lincoln*, because during the war the home-coming pilots used the highly-visible cathedral as a welcome navigational pointer. The Flight also has several Spitfires and Hurricanes, and various other aircraft.

You can visit them in their own hanger at a fully-operational RAF airfield. To avoid disappointment it is advisable to check by telephone which aircraft will be 'at home' as they are all operational and are often at airshows throughout the UK. There is a Visitor Centre, and one-hour tours with volunteer guides, usually ex-RAF.

Telephone number, see page 95. Open weekdays 10.00–17.00, last tour 15.30. Closed weekends, Bank Holidays, two weeks over Christmas. Admission charged.

Today

There are now four active military airfields in Lincolnshire, plus RAF Digby which is a listening station, and the Staff College at Cranwell.

RAF Coningsby, near Tattershall Bridge (map 8, page 49), is the nearest to the waterways in this guide. It was opened in November 1940 as a bomber airfield for No.5 Group. It has been operational ever since and 1984 saw the arrival of Tornado F2s.

By February 1988 the station was fully committed to Tornado operations and is now equipped with F3s. RAF Coningsby is on line to receive the first Eurofighter 2000 aircraft.

Weekdays are the best time to see the modern aircraft because in normal circumstances the RAF does not practice at week-ends. Look out for Tornadoes, strangely-shaped AWACs, and planes of NATO allies. On the other hand weekends are a good time to see the aircraft of the Battle of Britain Memorial Flight in the sky as they return home from air displays.

For telephone numbers of all of the above, see page 95.

Map 8: *River Witham*
Tattershall Bridge – Chapel Hill
2 miles

General Area
A busier section of the river. The old buildings attract nesting swallows, martins and barn owls, and in the summer swifts swoop low. However, the close proximity of RAF Coningsby also means that somewhat noisier flying objects are also in the sky here. The country road continues along one bank, and the A153 crosses at Tattershall Bridge. From here it is one mile to the town and a little further to the Battle of Britain Memorial Flight Visitor Centre. (See page 47).

This area is also covered on page 84.

Tattershall Bridge
Two bridges cross the river. The old one is late 18th century, its three red-brick arches built to carry a turnpike road. Now it is unused and the A153 crosses on the new bridge, opened in 1992.

Dogdyke Pumping Station
The livelihood of many Lincolnshire people depends on the efficient drainage of the fens. Most early pumps were wind powered and one such was built at Dogdyke in 1796. In 1856 a steam-powered beam engine and scoop-wheel was installed and these can still be seen. The huge boiler for the steam engine was floated down the river from Lincoln, and the coal to feed it also came by boat. In use until 1940 it was then replaced by the diesel engine in the adjacent building.

The old beam engine was restored by a Preservation Trust formed in 1973. There are demonstrations on open days, and a small museum with farmhouse refreshments. Open: May to October, on the first Sunday of each month, 14.00–17.00. (Telephone, see page 95).

Dogdyke
The outfall of the River Bain, flowing down from Horncastle. It was navigable up to that town but now only a few yards is used by boats going to Belle Isle Marina. It is a shorter walk to the *Battle of Britain Memorial Flight* if you arrange a mooring with either of the two pub landlords.

More details see the Horncastle Canal, page 84.

Chapel Hill
Moored boats line the last yards of the Slea Navigation's route down from Sleaford. At its junction with the Witham the rural sounds often include cuckoos, the wind whiffling, moorhens calling, and a chorus of bird song.
More details see the Slea Navigation, page 70.

Navigable Drains
The fens are not only land converted from marsh by drainage, but they are also a network of ditches which provide water for irrigation in dry seasons. For instance a supply for the Navigable Drains (pages 62-67) is taken from the River Witham, south of Dogdyke, through the bank opposite Orchard Caravans. When operating, water can be seen pouring through a modest concrete structure in the bank.

Navigation
Reduced Water Levels in Winter, and Mooring Prohibitions.
1st November to 1st April, see note, page 13.

Tattershall Bridge
Both bridges—navigation through centre arches.

Visitor Moorings, just downstream of bridges, modern pontoons, maximum stay 24hrs at one time. Rubbish skip by fishing tackle shop. Dogs must be kept on a lead. Traffic noise is minimal now that the old bridge is not used.

Tattershall. Around the village green are a small supermarket, newsagent, hairdresser, fish & chips, pub with food, cafe, bakery and telephone. More information, page 84.

Dogdyke
Belle Isle Marina. In the River Bain, at the rear of the Hornblower's pub. Moorings, toilets, slipway—by arrangement with the landlord (see advert page 51).

Orchard Caravans
Moorings for shop, heated swimming pool, bar meals, children's play area, fishing, Calor Gas. Boaters very welcome. (Telephone, see page 94).
Proprietors: Terry and Shirley Pollard.

Walking
The bank can be used past/through Orchard Caravans, it is not a public footpath but is well used by locals. At Chapel Hill a well-mown path goes along both sides of the Slea Navigation, allowing passage across the road bridge.

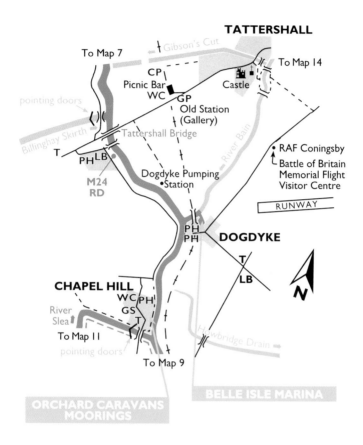

TATTERSHALL

To Map 7

Gibson's Cut

To Map 14

CP
Picnic Bar
WC

Castle

GP
Old Station
(Gallery)

pointing doors

Billinghay Skirth

River Bain

Tattershall Bridge

T

PH LB

M24
RD

Dogdyke Pumping
•Station

• RAF Coningsby
Battle of Britain
Memorial Flight
Visitor Centre

RUNWAY

PH
PH

DOGDYKE

T
LB

N

CHAPEL HILL

WC PH
GS
T

River
Slea

To Map 11

pointing doors

To Map 9

Howbridge Drain

BELLE ISLE MARINA

**ORCHARD CARAVANS
MOORINGS**

Dogdyke Pumping Station, Tattershall Castle in the background

Old Tattershall Bridge

Grazing the banks

Dogdyke

Map 9: *River Witham*
Chapel Hill – Langrick Bridge
5$\frac{1}{2}$ miles

General Area
The most remote stretch of the river. No roads come near, and beyond the floodbanks flat cultivated fields stretch for many miles. Semi-isolated houses and farms are dotted about, often with windbreak conifers or hedges. The distant roads are lined with a surprising number of lovely mature trees, many of them horse-chestnuts. Brown empty fields are rare, this is one of England's premier growing areas—onions, cabbages, beetroot, cereals, the dark green ridges of potatoes, the yellow of rape and the blue of flax.

Langrick Bridge
The girder road-bridge was built in 1907 as a replacement for a small flat-bed ferry.

Great Northern Railway
Its old track line runs along the north bank of the Witham between Lincoln and Boston. Opened in October 1848 it had stations at Bardney and Southrey. From November 1874 there was also a branch line from Bardney to Louth. In 1970 Bardney and Southrey stations closed to passengers, but goods trains served Bardney's sugar beet factory until 1981.

Plans are now underway to convert the route into a cycleway, see page 15.

Navigation
Reduced Water Levels in Winter, and Mooring Prohibitions.
1st November to 1st April, see note, page 13.

Langrick Bridge
No proper moorings. General store, post box, garage for petrol and red diesel.

Pontoon moorings have not been installed because they may require costly bank protection work.

Fishing Heritage. In the early 1900s the new railways made it possible for anglers from the industrial midlands and Yorkshire to travel to the Lincolnshire waterways. Special trains brought 500 for matches—it was good for the village traders but local residents complained of rough language, stolen garden flowers, work-stained clothes, and rowdiness.

It was a clash of cultures. For the city fishermen it was often a first visit to the peaceful countryside, a great change from the industrial din of their lives. They knew nothing of rural life and did not think clothes common in the city would be out of place elsewhere. The local people knew nothing of the visitors' working strains, nor their living conditions. To them they looked outlandish and alien.

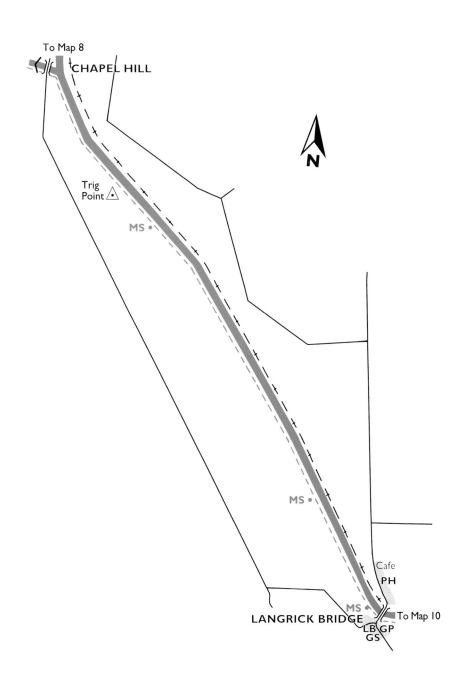

To Map 8

CHAPEL HILL

Trig
Point △

N

MS •

MS •

Cafe

PH

MS •

LANGRICK BRIDGE

To Map 10

LB GP
GS

Map 10: *River Witham*
Langrick Bridge – Boston (Grand Sluice)
4¹/₂ miles

General Area.
The isolated nature of the Witham continues until it undergoes a complete change for the final stretch to Boston.

Visiting boats line the north bank, on the opposite side are the craft of local boat clubs. The vital control function of the river's Grand Sluice soon becomes obvious. Upstream of the barrier the Witham is a controlled and benign waterway. Downstream it is the uncontrolled tidal link to the Wash, sometimes picturesque and sometimes nothing but banks of mud. The tide range here is usually up to 23ft, but it can go up to 28ft on exceptional tides. However, this may change as a sea lock is being studied to regulate the water levels through Boston.

Antons Gowt
Flanked by high stone walls this lock is the only entrance to the Witham Navigable Drains, and a second approach route to Boston. It is also one of the rare locations where boats lock *down* from a river.

The tower of Boston's famous parish church, its 'stump', can clearly be seen to the east.

Boston
(Town details, see page 58.)
Boston is well worth a visit, a busy market town, the capital of the fenlands, the social and supply centre for a vast agricultural area. In most towns the colourful vehicles for sale in roadside showrooms are cars—here they are tractors. The south bank is lined with houses of various designs, the town centre confined to the north bank.

A short distance downstream of the Grand Sluice, overlooking everything, is the famous 'stump' of the riverside parish church.

The current Town Bridge in the centre of Boston was completed in 1913. It replaced the original iron bridge which was built by John Rennie in 1806–1808. This was demolished in 1911 by the simple method of having the paddle-steamer *Privateer* pull it down.

Further downstream is the entrance to Boston's still thriving docks.

Navigation
If the wind is blowing upriver the straight stretch between Antons Gowt and the Grand Sluice at Boston can be a little choppy.

There may also be a large number of rowing skiffs between Antons Gowt and Boston. Please slow down and take care.

Reduced Water Levels in Winter, and Mooring Prohibitions.
1st November to 1st April, see note, page 13.

Antons Gowt
The only entrance to the Witham Navigable Drains, and a rare chance to cruise below sea level, and in the eastern hemisphere. (See pages 62-67).

There are moorings on the river, and BW is considering the installation of pontoons. In windy weather it is often more sheltered and pleasant to moor through the lock in the Drains, directly outside the adjacent pub.

Lock. Manual operation, with large gates, renewed in 1996. The change of level is down.

British Waterways' facilities
The furthest upstream jetties on the north bank are BW visitor moorings, further on are those of Boston Marina. On the south bank are the private moorings of Boston Motor Yacht Club.

The BW visitor moorings have an electricity hook-up service. A BW Watermate key is necessary to unlock a gate for the exit path into town. Charges payable to the lock-keeper at the Grand Sluice, £4.00 overnight.

Boston Marina
Diesel, overnight moorings, refuse disposal, elsan disposal, toilets, water. (Telephone, see page 94).

Boston Grand Sluice
Elsan disposal, refuse disposal, toilets, water, are available adjacent to the lock-keeper's cabin immediately above the Grand Sluice.

Passing through the Grand Sluice
See page 87.

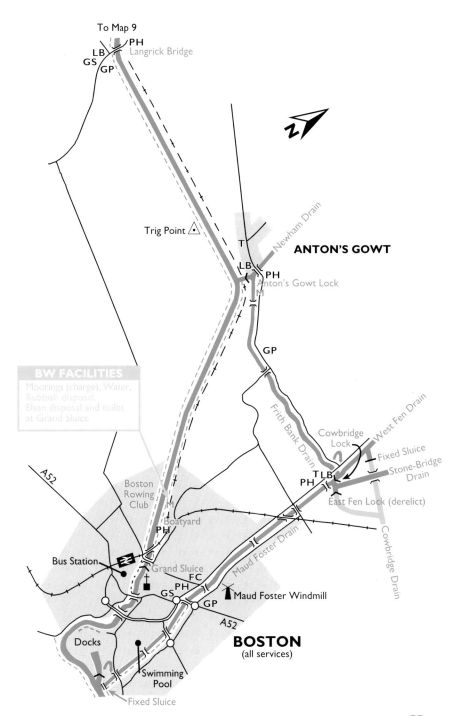

To Map 9

PH
LB
GS
GP
Langrick Bridge

Trig Point △

T
LB
PH
M
Anton's Gowt Lock

ANTON'S GOWT

Newham Drain

GP

Frith Bank Drain

West Fen Drain

Cowbridge Lock

Fixed Sluice

Stone-Bridge Drain

T LB
PH

East Fen Lock (derelict)

Cowbridge Drain

BW FACILITIES
Moorings (charge), Water,
Rubbish disposal,
Elsan disposal and toilet
at Grand Sluice

A52

Boston
Rowing
Club

M

Boatyard

PH

Maud Foster Drain

Bus Station

Grand Sluice

FC

GS
PH

GP

A52

Maud Foster Windmill

Docks

Swimming
Pool

Fixed Sluice

BOSTON
(all services)

55

Grand sluice viewed from The Stump

Boston

Visitor moorings at Boston

Fishing fleet viewed in The Haven

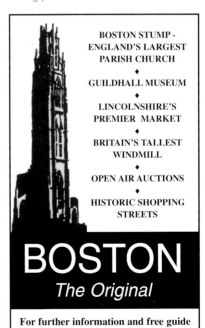

Boston

One advantage of being a river-based visitor to Boston is that it is always possible to find the way back to the water. The towering presence of 'The Stump' can be seen all over town—and the church is by the river.

Boston is first and foremost a market town, the tradition of which goes back to 1308. Then the town was this country's second port and traders from all over England and the Low Countries came to sell their goods.

Market days. A traditional street market on Wednesdays and Saturdays, with Wednesday having the added bonus of an open-air auction on The Green in Wide Bargate. Here anything can be bought, from eggs and plants to a bicycle, but the bidding is fast and furious.

May Fair. In 1545 Henry VIII granted Boston a charter which allowed an annual fair to be held in the Market Place and it still takes place. Now it is a week long fun-fair which fills the entire centre of the town in the first week of May.

Reminders of a *maritime past* abound in the southern section of the High Street. A plaque by the Crown & Anchor notes the home of George Bass 1771–1803 who discovered Bass Strait and played a significant part in the history of Tasmania, and the Australian state of Victoria. The Old Ship Inn, and Boston Boats chandlery overlook the moorings of today's mussel fleet. The area around South Street was once a bustling quay and the old Custom House, the second oldest in England, has the royal coat of arms over the door.

Boston has not lost its links with the sea, on the southern edge of the town the seven acres of *docks* opened in 1884 are still busy with container ships up to 3,000 tonnes, usually from western Europe. There is a footpath on the bank opposite the entrance lock but shipping activity is tide dependant.

St Botolph's is the largest parish church in England. Built in the 14th century it is affectionately known as 'The Stump'. The distinctive tower is 272 feet high, and from it there are panoramic views of Lincolnshire and the Wash. The reason for the tower's shape is not known, some say it was never completed and that a spire was intended to top it. The church is open every day, 0900—1630, but the tower is closed on Sundays. For safety reasons visitors under 18 climbing the tower must be accompanied by an adult. (Telephone, see page 95).

American Connections. Boston has strong links with America because of its early association with the group who later sailed to the New World and became known as the Pilgrim Fathers. Large numbers of Boston citizens travelled to America, five of them becoming

Governors of Massachusetts with an active involvement in the new town bearing the name of Boston.

Windmills are part of Lincolnshire's history and there were many in the Boston area. The restored *Maud Foster windmill* stands alongside Boston's second waterway approach, the similarly named Drain. (See page 61).

Guildhall Museum. In South Street, built 1450. Now a museum of Boston and its maritime heritage. The Maritime Room contains reminders of Boston's history of trading, seafaring and boat-building. Court Room, cells (best known as where the Pilgrim Fathers were imprisoned in 1607 and put on trial), banqueting hall, council chamber, and 17th century kitchens. Monday to Saturday, 10.00—17.00. Sunday (summer only) 13.30—17.00. (Telephone, see page 95).

The *Sam Newsom Music Centre* in South Street was formerly a seed warehouse, one of the many that lined the river. It has been carefully converted to preserve the outward appearance but inside it is the Music Department of Boston College and a number of concerts are held in the magnificent recital hall.

The *Havenside Country Park* extends from the Maud Foster Drain eastwards along the north bank of the Witham's tidal section, to the mud-flats of the Wash and the coastal path. It is still under development but it passes the Pilgrim Fathers' Memorial and has interesting riverside and seabank walks.

Boat Trips
Maritime Leisure Cruises, Wed & Sun, 1hr, leaves from Sluice Bridge. Also other river and Wash cruises. Groups made up from individuals if necessary.

Adventure Afloat—day-boat hire on the Witham above the Grand Sluice. (Telephone, see page 94).

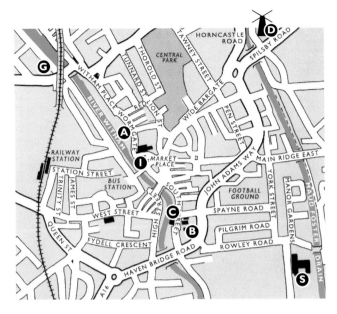

A St Botolph's Church/Stump
B Guildhall Museum
C Sam Newson Music Centre
D Maud Foster Windmill

G Grand Sluice
I Tourist Information
S Swimming Pool

Heading down the tideway

Parish Church of St Botolph (The Stump)

Maud Foster Windmill stands alongside Maud Foster Drain

Cowbridge Lock and Stonebridge Drain

Operating the guillotine gate, Cowbridge Lock

The Navigable Drains

The fenlands, of which the Drains are an integral part, have a continuity of landscape across their fine soil of great fertility. These flat lands are below sea level and there is an absence of hedges, instead the network of Drains marks the field boundaries. There are also few established villages, instead the scattered farms and cottages sometimes huddle together into small settlements.

In the middle ages sheep were reared in the fens, primarily for their wool which was England's most important source of wealth at that time. The fens were also used for growing hay and reeds, for fishing, and occasionally as ploughed land. These activities promoted interest and landowners started to enclose areas by digging drainage ditches, a pattern still seen today.

In the late middle ages there was a decline in the wool trade and fenlands became neglected, including the Drains. Before long the area was said to be virtually worthless, but the inhabitants did not agree. They made a reasonable living from grazing rights, wild fowling, and fishing.

With the coming of the Industrial Revolution there was a need for increased agricultural production and in 1762 an Act of Parliament was obtained to authorise major drainage works in the area of the River Witham. Also included was the setting up of six *Internal Drainage Districts*. Each of the six was to be controlled as an independent area, separated one from the other by a system of flood banks and sluice gates. The theory was similar to that of watertight compartments in a ship—if breaches, downpours, or pump failures inundated one low-lying area the damage would be contained without spreading to neighbouring Districts. That is why some of the navigable Drains are still controlled by the *Witham Fourth District Internal Drainage Board*.

Vast capital investments were made in the fens, the objective being to convert grassland, only useful for six months, into land which could support farming all the year round. But even with such efforts the changeover was not easy, it took time. The early crops were only oats and clover but eventually the fields produced wheat, barley, turnips, beans, peas, chicory, mustard, hemp and flax.

Flooding was, however, still a danger, especially in the winter if the River Witham was swollen with melting snow. Because the fens are so low-lying, pumps have always been necessary to raise unwanted water up to the River Witham. In the 18th century windmills powered such pumps but after the 1820s steam power was often installed. More powerful and reliable they made a great difference to the fenlands. Eventually the steam engines were replaced by diesel power, and now electric motors do most of the work. Many of the present pumping stations are on the sites of their hard-working predecessors.

Each summer the drains are used to store water for irrigation purposes. The lowland system is filled in the spring of each year from the River Witham at Antons Gowt, and subsequently augmented with transfers at Dogdyke, see page 48.

Windmills are part of Lincolnshire's history and there were many in the Boston area. The restored *Maud Foster windmill* stands alongside the similarly named Drain at Boston. It is Britain's tallest working mill and has seven floors to which visitors may climb to see milling in progress. During the 1900s the adjacent Drain was used by corn barges bringing grain from the surrounding fens to the mill for grinding. The mill works daily, when the wind blows, producing stoneground organic flour which, with other items, can be purchased during mill opening hours. All year: Wednesday 10.00—17.00; Sundays and Bank Holidays 14.00—17.00. (Telephone, see page 95).

Sibsey Trader windmill. One of the very few six-sailed mills remaining in England. It was built in 1877 in typical Lincolnshire style with a tapering brick tower, tarred outside, white-washed within, and a white-painted wooden cap. The machinery is still intact and wooden ladders can be climbed to all six floors to see the whole process on the special milling days. Bags of freshly milled flour can be purchased. Wheelchair access to the ground floor only. Toilets, car park. English Heritage. (Telephone, see page 95).

Navigation. The primary usage of the Drains has always been water removal and storage but they were also an obvious means of transport. Farming families used boats to go into Boston for the markets, to sell their produce and to buy what could not be grown. From that time the right of navigation has been maintained on the larger Drains although drainage and irrigation are always the priority functions.

Madeley Wood *on Newham Drain, north of Westville*

Wigford *crosses West Fen Drain at Westville*

Anton's Gowt Lock, entrance to the Witham Navigable Drains—note the gauging board on the corner of the wall

Quiet mooring outside the Oak Tree public house

The Navigable Drains

Navigation

Of the 90 miles of man-made waterways north of Boston approximately 40 miles remain navigable. The Drains are a world of their own, one of the few places where a cruise on a hot August bank holiday can be completed without seeing another craft. Nevertheless they are an acquired taste—some find them remote and boring, others find them remote and peaceful. At least give them a try.

Narrowboats are most suited to the Drains but owners of low-headroom cruisers may also wish to visit. The passage along Frith Bank Drain to Cowbridge Lock, and then perhaps along the tree-lined Maud Foster to Boston, is a simple cruise. An alternative straight-forward circular route, from Cowbridge Lock, is north along the West Fen Drain through Frithville to Westville, returning southwards on the Newham Drain to Antons Gowt.

But be careful, some get bitten by the 'explorer' bug and never rest until every nook and cranny has been ticked off. An obsession perhaps, but at least they can truthfully say they have cruised to New York. If nothing else, the Drains are a rare opportunity on Britain's inland waterways to lock down from a river, and to cruise in the eastern hemisphere. Perhaps a 'crossing the line' ceremony on the Stonebridge Drain at the Greenwich Meridian!

Water levels/bridge heights

Because drainage and irrigation have priority over navigation it is wise when entering the Drains at Antons Gowt to check the water level on the **gauging board** on the tail wall of the lock. The normal summer reading is shown as '0'. The bridge heights on the map reflect this base level.

Conditions depend on the seasons and the weather. After or during wet seasons the Drains may be kept at a low level to aid drainage. But in a dry summer they act as storage areas for irrigation water and may therefore be kept at a high level.

It is also wise to check with the Witham Fourth District Internal Drainage Board before going too deep into the system. There is a telephone box 400 yds from Antons Gowt Lock, and by Cowbridge Lock. (Telephone, see page 94).

Cowbridge lock

Dimensions, see page 12. The guillotine gate at the top is unlocked with a BW Watermate key. The bottom gates are unusual in having no balance-beams, instead they are opened by pulling on chains. Leave the lock with its gates and paddles closed, and the guillotine door in the fully down position, and padlocked.

Head of Navigation Plaque

A plaque is available for photographic proof of a craft passing through Cowbridge Lock. From Mr D Carnell, Conifer Cottage, Northend, Goxhill, North Lincolnshire DN19 7JX. £6.00, inc p&p, cheques payable to the Inland Waterways Association.

Facilities

There are no specific moorings or water-points, or any other facilities on the Drains. Be prepared.

Eastern Drains

It used to be possible to cross the Stonebridge Drain and descend a further lock to the eastern Drains, but East Fen Lock is now disused.

Maud Foster, and West Fen Catchwater Drains

Although their land-drainage function is controlled by the Environment Agency the body responsible for navigation is unclear. Therefore, boat owners must ensure that during the winter their craft are securely attended to or removed from these strategic waterways so that they do not pose a problem during times of flood.

A fixed sluice at Boston means there is no access to/from the River Witham via the Maud Foster Drain.

Ken Barber, foreman of the Witham Fourth Internal Drainage Board, is the person who best knows the Drains. If you have the opportunity to talk to Ken, take it. (Telephone, see page 94).

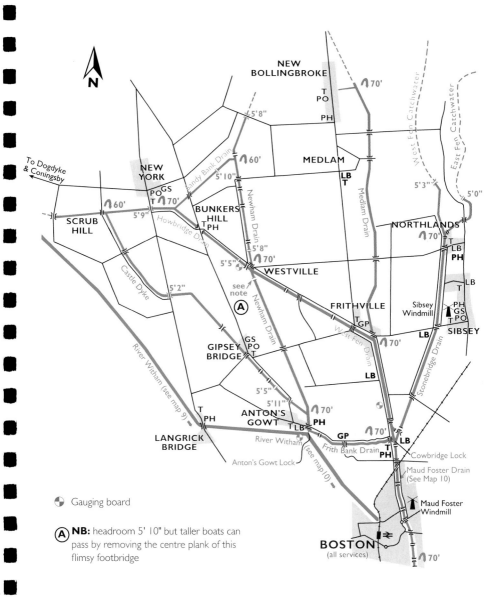

Map labels

NEW BOLLINGBROKE
T
PO
PH
↑70'

5'8"

↑60'
MEDLAM
LB
T
5'10"

NEW YORK
PO GS
T ↑70'

West Fen Catchwater
East Fen Catchwater

5'3"
5'0"

↑60'
SCRUB HILL
5'9"

Sandy Bank Drain
Newham Drain
Howbridge Drain

BUNKERS HILL
T PH
5'8"
↑70'

NORTHLANDS
↑70'
LB
PH

Castle Dyke

5'2"

5'5"
see note
(A)

WESTVILLE

Medlam Drain

T
LB

Sibsey Windmill

PH
GS
PO
T

Newham Drain

FRITHVILLE
T GP

LB
SIBSEY

West Fen Drain

↑70'

GIPSEY BRIDGE
GS PO T

River Witham (see map 9)

Stonebridge Drain

LB

5'5"
5'11"
↑70'
PH

ANTON'S GOWT
T LB
GP

↑70'
LB

T
PH
↑70'

Cowbridge Lock

T PH

LANGRICK BRIDGE

River Witham (see map 0)

Frith Bank Drain

Maud Foster Drain (See Map 10)

Anton's Gowt Lock

Maud Foster Windmill

To Dogdyke & Coningsby

🌓 Gauging board

(A) **NB:** headroom 5' 10" but taller boats can pass by removing the centre plank of this flimsy footbridge

BOSTON
(all services)

↑70'

Moorings at Chapel Hill

Pointing Doors

Slea Navigation

History of the Slea Navigation

The River Slea is a typical anonymous Lincolnshire waterway until it reaches Sleaford. Downstream of the small town the river splits into the Old Slea and the New Slea.

As its name suggests the Old Slea is thought to be the original course of the river. The origin of the New Slea is not known, it may be man-made or natural, but it was used by boats as early as 1342, mainly for tolls to keep the banks in good repair, ever important in flat Lincolnshire.

Throughout the centuries the primary functions of the New Slea were land drainage and driving water-mills, but the canal boom of the late 18th century changed all that.

Canal Boom

A canal between Sleaford and Grantham was proposed in 1774 but there was more interest in making the New Slea navigable to the already improved River Witham.

In the 1770s and 1780s conflicting local interests halted any progress. The farmers were effective in their protests, successfully petitioning Parliament against the scheme because they feared they would no longer be able to water their cattle from the waterway. A further problem was the high toll charge made by the Witham Commissioners on their river; the costs a hindrance to through traffic to the Slea. Eventually the problems were resolved and a survey by the famous engineer William Jessop in 1792 became the basis for the authorising Act of Parliament.

The idea was to share resources with the nearby Horncastle Canal scheme. One engineer was to be in charge of the construction of both waterways but when the chosen man, Henry Eastburn, was delayed by an unfinished project, the Slea Navigation Company decided to go ahead on its own.

John Jagger of Gainsborough was appointed Engineer and various contractors did the work on the locks and bridges. The proposed town terminus and wharf would have meant continuing through Sleaford but a less ambitious plan was implemented because of inadequate funding. The waterway did however reach to the base of Money's Mill which still stands in the town centre and houses the Tourist Information office.

Navigation Opened

Many of Sleaford's traders made considerable investments in the scheme. A totally new watercourse was unnecessary, instead the New Slea was straightened and deepened so that large boats could reach the town. It took two years to complete the work and the Slea Navigation was officially opened on May 6th 1794.

Throughout its trading years two cargoes dominated on the Slea: outward; corn and milled grain from the surrounding area, and inward; coal from Yorkshire and Derbyshire.

For the first 15 trading years the Navigation made a loss, but it was supported by local commercial interests because its beneficial effect on trade compensated for the operating losses. An example was the restoration to profitability of Cogglesford water-mill which, prior to the navigation, was restricted to working only eight hours a day because river water was extracted by upstream landowners.

The major restriction suffered by the waterway during its early years was that boats were delayed by navigational problems on the River Witham. These were alleviated by major works from 1808-1812, after which Slea prospered.

Railways

The Slea's most prosperous period was in the 1840s but it was not to last. After 1849 a new railway from Peterborough to Lincoln and Boston took some trade from the Navigation but there was worse to come. A few years later another line from Grantham to Boston, via Sleaford, was far more damaging.

Boat traffic decreased rapidly, tolls fell, maintenance was delayed and the waterway silted up. Local traders fearing a railway monopoly kept the Navigation going for a few years, but the Company was eventually wound up in 1881. The waterway went back to its drainage role, with navigation only kept open on the lower reaches until the 1930s.

Sleaford Navigation Society

The turning point was the formation of the Sleaford Navigation Society in 1977, as a result of its efforts Bottom Lock was reopened in 1986 and major works undertaken at Cobblers Lock.

In 1996 a regeneration grant was awarded to improve the waterway at Sleaford and the top lock, as well as saving the old offices of the Navigation Company. Funding is now being sought from the Millennium Commission to restore the Slea to full navigation standard throughout.

Map 11: *Slea Navigation*
Chapel Hill – Cobblers Lock
7$\frac{1}{2}$ miles

General Area
At the confluence of the Slea and Witham it is normally fresh and breezy, even in very hot weather. Both banks up to the road bridge are lined with moored boats, the bank topped with a neatly mown path. The lower miles of the River Slea are through typical Lincolnshire countryside, with only two villages marking its course. Above Bottom Lock the ability to see over the floodbanks is welcome after the relative confines of the River Witham.

Navigation of the Slea was abandoned by Act of Parliament in 1878 but the occupants of the Haverholme estate (map 12, page 75) maintained the usage of the river from the estate to the Witham for their own use. This continued until 1930, so the lower reaches of the Slea were in a better condition than the rest when the *Sleaford Navigation Society* was founded in 1977 and restoration planning commenced.

Names to confuse matters the lower reaches of the River Slea, between Chapel Hill and South Kyme, are locally referred to as the Kyme Eau.

Chapel Hill
A small, quiet village. A stone balustraded bridge crosses the Slea, the centre of its arch marked as the border between two of Lincolnshire's historic district divisions, Kesteven and Holland. House martins nest under the bridge in the summer and the air is full of their twittering and swooping flight.

South Kyme
The Sleaford Navigation Society's annual festival is held in the village, at which time the waterway is lined with boats. On the riverside the *South Kyme Archway* commemorates the Navigation's 200th anniversary. The images reflect various aspects, including fish swimming, and a kingfisher.

The rather neat church is the surviving fragment of a great Augustinian Priory founded here some time before 1169.

South Kyme Tower
77 feet high, built between 1340 and 1380, probably as part of a castle. It has four floors and battlements and was used as part of the earlier manor house on the site.

Cobblers Lock
The chamber walls have been completely dismantled and rebuilt by the Sleaford Navigation Society. However, the gates will not be installed until agreement has been reached with the Environment Agency about the resultant water levels on the section above the lock.

Navigation
Navigation of the Slea is not permitted between 1 November and 1 April—the gates of Bottom Lock are padlocked open to aid land drainage. At all times water levels may fluctuate, and the Slea can be very weedy in late summer. Cruisers should note the restrictive 6ft 6ins air draught of the downstream bridge at South Kyme.

Chapel Hill
The 'pointing door' flood gates by the road bridge are only closed when the Witham is higher than the Slea. Leave as found.

Bridge Farm
Beware of wooden piles of old bridge.

Bottom Lock
Dimensions, see page 12. Guillotine top gate requires lots of turns. Standard windlass.

South Kyme
It is possible to turn a 30ft craft at the village, otherwise it is necessary to go on to Cobblers Lock.

Cobblers Lock
Current head of navigation, 70ft turning point in the river mouth just below. Restoration planned for above.

Head of Navigation Plaque
A plaque is available for photographic proof of craft reaching the head of navigation, currently Cobblers Lock. From Mrs P Taylor, 26 Park Lane, Heighington, Lincoln LN4 1RF. £7.00 inc p&p, cheques payable to Sleaford Navigation Society.

Walking
Between South Kyme and Cobblers Lock the path may become overgrown in mid-summer.

The Slea is one of the walks in the *Stepping Out* series, leaflet from Sleaford Tourist Information. (Telephone, see page 95).

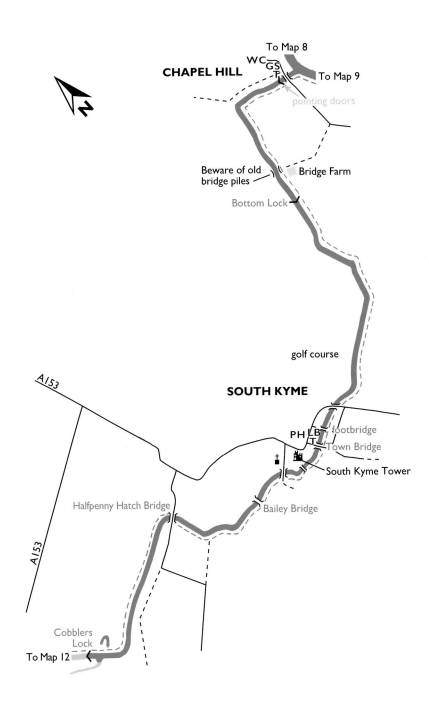

To Map 8

WC
GS

CHAPEL HILL

To Map 9

pointing doors

Beware of old
bridge piles

Bridge Farm

Bottom Lock

golf course

A153

SOUTH KYME

footbridge

PH LB

Town Bridge

South Kyme Tower

Halfpenny Hatch Bridge

A153

Bailey Bridge

Cobblers
Lock

To Map 12

TIMBERLAND PUMPING STATION
& TALES OF THE RIVERBANK

Situated on the banks of the River Witham, the pumping station was built in 1839 to drain 2,500 acres of fenland marsh so that it could be used for farming. You can see the pump and engine (working on special open days) and many of the original tools and technical documents used.

The "Tales of the Riverbank" exhibition, in a small purpose-built visitor centre, tells how the fen was formed and of the lives of those who inhabited this area.

OPEN: May-October: Wednesday-Sunday 2-5. November-April: Saturday & Sunday 1-4

ADMISSION: Free

LOCATION: On the river bank on the minor road off the A155 to Louth and Skegness which runs between Kirkstead Bridge and Tatershall Bridge.

For further information please contact: Sleaford Tourist Information, The Mill, Money's Yard, Carre Street, Sleaford, Lincs NG34 7TW or Telephone: 01529 414294

South Kyme Tower

Bottom Lock was restored by the Sleaford Navigation Society

Toll booth at Corn Mill Lock

Haverholme Lock

Map 12: *Slea Navigation*
Cobblers Lock – Sleaford
4½ miles

General Area

Between Cobblers lock and Sleaford there are two waterways—the Old Slea, and the New Slea. Their history is obscure but this guide follows the New Slea because it was, and at some time will be again, the navigable channel.

Above Cobblers Lock is rural and the solitude is wonderful. The Slea is narrow, with high banks which lessen as progress is made upstream. Beyond the towpath is the start of the Lincolnshire prairies, great grain acres spreading to the edge of sight. The land is still not quite flat as this is the edge of the real fenlands. Farms and a few trees break the horizon. Birds splash away, not used to being disturbed. Sit quietly at Cobblers Lock and there are all sorts of sounds—scufflings, splashings, bird calls, water running over the weir.

Many of the locks bear the names of the once adjacent mills which used the change in water level as a power source.

In the droughts of a few summers ago the Slea was one of the ten driest rivers in Britain but remedial work has alleviated the situation to some degree.

Haverholme Lock

Downstream of the road bridge the towpath is nicely mown and the area is very pleasant. The date 1893 is marked on the keystone of the elaborate bridge. Between the bridge and the lock, views of the canal from the towpath are sometimes obscured by summer vegetation, but the shell of Haverholme Priory can be seen across the fields.

Paper Mill Lock

A quiet place with hardly any traffic in the lane. Flat corn fields are all around, beyond which rise tree-lined ridges. The lock's name comes from Evedon Paper Mill, which used to be lockside. Its seven sets of millstones made paper for a Boston printing works.

Corn Mill Lock

The long red building was once Holdingham Mill, until 1957 producing flour for local bakers and fish fryers. It is now a private residence, in the garden of which can be seen a small octagonal building which was originally a tollbooth for the navigation.

In the summer roses grow over the edge of the lock chamber edge, and swallows and martins line the overhead wires.

Bone Mill Lock

The mill here produced fertiliser by crushing animal bones.

Cogglesford Mill

Carefully restored in 1993 the mill turned again under water power for the first time in 108 years. The name refers to an ancient 'coggle' or cobbled ford, a few yards downstream on the Slea.

Admission and parking free. Opening times, Easter–Oct, daily 10.00–17.00. Nov–Easter, Sat and Sun, 10.00–16.00.

(Telephone, see page 95).

Beside the mill is the lock chamber. The wide area of water above is the mill-pond, built as a reservoir when the Slea was made navigable, supplying a head of water to drive the mill even if some of it was used for the lock.

Sleaford

On the final approach to the town the navigable Slea divided into two channels, now a grassed area.

The bridges in Carre Street over what were the navigation's two arms were formally swing bridges. Further along the same street there is a 'Navigation Wharf' portal on a building although this is not its original site.

However, the greatest gem is a little further towards the town centre along Carre Street. In a yard is the old office building of the Canal Company, its arms still over the door. It was built in 1838 and funding for its restoration has been obtained.

Navigation

Currently un-navigable above Cobblers Lock, but the Sleaford Navigation Society is campaigning for full restoration.

Walking

The towpath tends to be hummocky.

At Anwick access to the towpath is from the bottom of River Lane.

Near Sleaford there is a path under the A17, just to the east of the waterway, via steps and stiles.

There is no towpath under the railway bridge, but follow the path to pass under nearby.

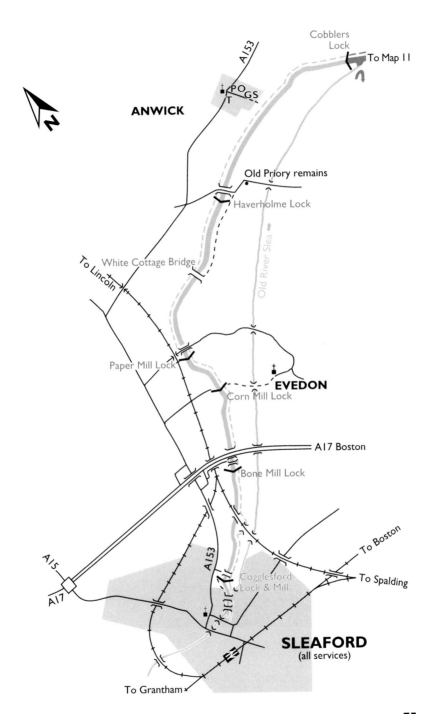

Cobblers
Lock

To Map 11

A153

† P O GS
T

ANWICK

Old Priory remains

Haverholme Lock

White Cottage Bridge

To Lincoln

Old River Slea

Paper Mill Lock

EVEDON

Corn Mill Lock

A17 Boston

Bone Mill Lock

A15

A153

A17

To Boston

To Spalding

Cogglesford
Lock & Mill

SLEAFORD
(all services)

To Grantham

75

Navigation House

Cogglesford Mill

Sleaford

A settlement since Saxon times, by 1066 Sleaford was established as an administrative centre for the region. Through the years it grew as a commercial centre with the River Slea powering eighteen mills.

A market has been held since Anglo-Saxon times and now takes place on Mondays, Fridays, and Saturdays.

As well as the market there are many shops and large stores. Prominent in the town is the parish church of St Denys, with its tower dating from c.1180.

On Southgate there are two old inns. The White Hart has a stone held tablet with the date 1691, and the Black Bull has a unique sign on its wall dating from 1689, thought to be the oldest such inn sign in Britain.

The Maltings. Just south of Sleaford, an example of imposing industrial architecture, nationally famous, and built between 1892 and 1905 by the brewers Bass. The complex has eight pavilions, with a central tower from which a pump raised water from an artesian well 130 feet down, for the malting process.

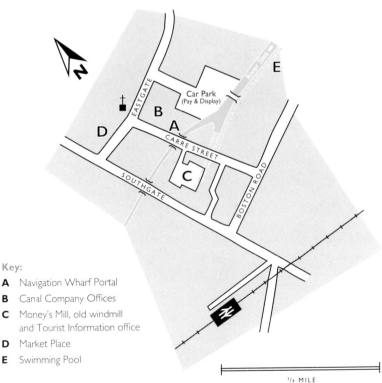

Key:

A Navigation Wharf Portal

B Canal Company Offices

C Money's Mill, old windmill and Tourist Information office

D Market Place

E Swimming Pool

History of the Horncastle Canal

In common with many other small towns, Horncastle saw the Canal Age of the late 18th century as a way of ending a semi-isolated existence. The atrocious roads limited trade to an area within ten miles, the distance people could travel to market and return home in one day, but a waterway link to the River Witham would change all that.

Experience elsewhere had also shown that such a project could also lessen the frequent flooding which plagued the town and the land to the south. Horncastle is at the confluence of the unpredictable rivers Bain and Waring and their joint waters often overflowed the land downstream.

An example of the benefits brought by a navigable waterway was easy to find. In 1786 a short private canal was constructed from Tattershall down to the River Witham. It was the work of two general merchants, John Gibson of Tattershall and John Dyson of Bawtry, the latter supplying the engineering experience. Known as Gibson's Cut, or the Tattershall Canal, it was only one mile long with one lock but it did show what could be accomplished and the trading advantages that were to be gained.

Jessop

In 1791 the famous engineer William Jessop judged that making the Bain navigable would be more cost-effective than building a new canal, although it had to be accepted that water resources would always need careful management because of the river's erratic flow pattern.

As in most other waterway schemes in Lincolnshire the driving force behind the planned Horncastle Canal was the powerful Sir Joseph Banks. (See page 18). His country seat was the nearby Revesby Abbey and he was owner or lease-holder of large tracts of land through which the new canal would pass.

With the considerable backing of Jessop and Sir Joseph Banks the parliamentary Act authorising construction of the Horncastle Canal was passed on June 11th 1792, the same day as that for Sleaford's navigation, the twin scheme on the opposite bank of the Witham.

Canal Mania

The great popularity of waterway projects at that time made obtaining the Act and raising funds relatively easy. However, the number of schemes underway all over the country also meant that competent engineers were already fully employed. Jessop had planned the new waterway but he did not think it needed his personal attention after that. At the height of canal mania Horncastle's little canal had nothing to attract experienced men away from more prestigious schemes.

Eventually Henry Eastburn was chosen and he was also to accept responsibility for the work on the Slea Navigation. However, in November 1792 Eastburn was tempted elsewhere and the Horncastle Canal's construction problems began.

Incompetence

A succession of engineers were appointed, one of whom, William Cawley, used up two-thirds of the Canal Company's money before being dismissed for incompetent work. Jessop spent more time than he intended inspecting badly constructed locks, bridges and weirs.

By 1797 the canal had reached Dalderby, two miles short of its destination but lack of funds halted the work. It was a further five years before the canal was completed to Horncastle, a second Act allowing more money to be raised. Also the influence of Sir Joseph Banks secured the services of John Rennie, a young but well thought of civil engineer destined to take a place in the top ranks of his profession.

Rennie said the last two miles of the river Bain were too narrow and winding for navigation and he recommended a separate cut between Dalderby and Horncastle. This work, and the whole Horncastle Canal scheme, was completed in 1802. The cost was £45,000, nearly four times the original estimate.

Nevertheless, the canal linked Horncastle to the national trading network and the small market town thrived, helped by the fact that the locks were large enough to take the sloops and keels which came along the Witham from the Midlands and Yorkshire. Varied cargoes flowed in both directions but principally: outward; corn and milled grain, and inward; coal.

Railway

In 1855 Horncastle's first railway was opened and it was serious competition for the canal. By the 1870s much of the traffic had ceased. The last recorded cargo was on May 11th 1878, to Horncastle from Boston. The last meeting of the Canal Company was in 1884, and by 1889 the navigable waterway was abandoned.

One hundred years later the restoration of the Horncastle Canal is being discussed as a distinct possibility in the late 1990s.

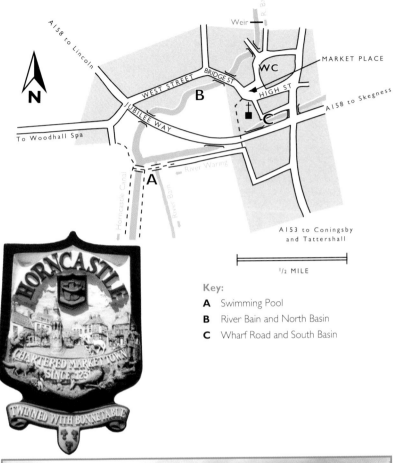

Key:

A Swimming Pool
B River Bain and North Basin
C Wharf Road and South Basin

Horncastle Market Place

Map13: *Horncastle Canal*
Horncastle – Kirkby-on-Bain
5¹/₂ miles

General Area
The Canal follows the course of the River Bain, and actually merges with it for long stretches downstream of Dalderby.

The countryside is the gently rolling foothills of the Lincolnshire wold, but still with acres of farmland in all directions.

The area around Kirkby-on-Bain is rich in gravel laid down in the last Ice Age. The huge lakes south of the village are old flooded gravel pits.

Horncastle
A thriving market town. It was once famous for its Horse Fair but today's attraction is the large number of antique shops. The popular markets are on Thursdays and Saturdays.

Horncastle's location below the hills of the Lincolnshire wold means that it is prone to flood if there is heavy sudden rain on those hills. The rivers Bain and Waring then find it difficult to cope with the volume of water and at their confluence in Horncastle the flood threat is doubled. In July 1996 there was 8ins of water in the streets but the last catastrophe was in 1960. The flood levels of that year are marked in Wharf Road, alongside the old south basin of the canal.

Troublesome though the rivers can be, they are the reason for the town's foundation. The Romans recognised the natural defensive site formed by the Bain and the Waring and their settlement was called Banovallum. Now the town is mainly 18th and 19th century with the King's Head one of a few remaining mud and stud buildings.

Dalderby
The Canal was built northwards from the River Witham and until 1802 Dalderby was the busy head of navigation. Goods were sent by road between here and Horncastle. After that date extra funds were found to build the last stretch of the canal to its name town—starting at the lock, the remains of which can still clearly be seen. There is a stone lock chamber with bottom gate recesses and the cut-off remains of top ground-paddle gear. The access path from the road is by the war-memorial, with a public footpath sign, then through a gate to meadowland. The head of navigation wharf was just below the lock, but there is no sign of it now, although the old river ford which gave access to it is still used by farm animals.

The Navigation Farmhouse by the road lay-by was built as the wharfinger's home.

Kirkby-on-Bain
The Canal Company had a large warehouse and wharf here. Sand and gravel, obtained nearby, continued as a major part of boat cargoes until the canal closed.

A watermill and sluices have been restored but they are difficult to see. Nearby the remains of an old lock are in the field behind a kennels establishment.

Navigation
The Horncastle Canal is un-navigable, although restoration plans are being discussed. The Lincolnshire branch of the Inland Waterways Association is lobbying local Councils to obtain funds for an initial feasibility study. (Telephone, see page 94).

Walking/Cycling
There is no continuous path along the Canal. From Horncastle it is possible to follow either bank to Thornton. The Viking Way/Spa Way comes alongside the canal downstream of Thornton, using the path of an old railway track which may also be used by bicycles.

There are circular walks in the Kirkby-on-Bain/Haltham area, and a leaflet is available from Horncastle Tourist Information, see page 95.

Remains of Kirkby Lock

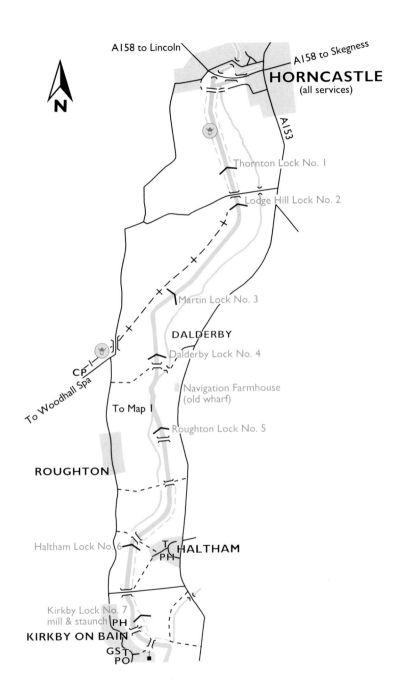

A158 to Lincoln

A158 to Skegness

HORNCASTLE
(all services)

A153

Thornton Lock No. 1

Lodge Hill Lock No. 2

Martin Lock No. 3

DALDERBY

Dalderby Lock No. 4

Navigation Farmhouse
(old wharf)

CP

To Woodhall Spa

To Map 1

Roughton Lock No. 5

ROUGHTON

Haltham Lock No. 6

T
PH **HALTHAM**

Kirkby Lock No. 7
mill & staunch
PH

KIRKBY ON BAIN

GS T
PO

N

North Basin, Horncastle

Navigation Farmhouse, Dalderby

Coningsby Church and single handed clock

Tattershall Castle and Church

Map14: *Horncastle Canal*
Kirkby-on-Bain – Dogdyke
5¹/₂ miles

General Area

A rich arable farming area, at the southern end of which Tattershall Castle and church are often noticeable on the skyline.

The canalised River Bain is prone to flood badly and quickly—after torrential rainfall it has trouble taking high volumes of water from the hills above Horncastle down to the River Witham. For this reason the canal locks have generally been weired where the top gates should be, with flow controls nearby. The last bad floods were in 1960, but some Horncastle houses were inundated in 1993 and 1996.

Near Fulsby lock is a peaceful area, the breeze carrying the cries of flocks of water birds on the gravel-pit lakes.

The Dogdyke area is also covered on page 48.

Coningsby

The River Bain is the border between Coningsby and Tattershall.

From the towpath the village is dominated by the church tower. Its single-handed clock is 16ft 6ins in diameter, claimed to be the world's largest working antique one-handed type still in existence.

The bridge carrying the A153 bridge over the river was reconstructed in 1962 because the previous one collapsed after Horncastle's last major flood swept beneath it on October 7th 1960.

Tattershall

The tree-shaded village green is surrounded by mostly 18–19th century buildings. They include the Fortescue Arms although a beam inside is dated 1623. On a ridge-tile of Lodge House is *'Tom Thumb's House'*, a device to ward off evil spirits from the main building by tempting them to enter this miniature house instead. The Market Cross (or Butter Cross) is thought to have been erected in the 15th century by Ralph, Lord Cromwell who was Henry VI's Treasurer of England.

Tattershall Castle

Dominating the small town is the castle's unique tower completed c1440 as an extension to an existing fortress. It is not built of stone as usually seen but instead is a rare example of a medieval brick fortification.

From the battlements there are magnificent views on clear days, including Boston's 'Stump'

and Lincoln Cathedral and RAF Coningsby is a fascinating sight for plane spotters.

National Trust, (Telephone, see page 95).

Gibson's Cut

This short canal, linking Tattershall to the River Witham, was built before the Horncastle Canal. It was a private venture and its success prompted the promotion of the later waterway.

The junction with the River Witham is now blocked by an embankment, and the first lock has been infilled. It is retained as a reservoir for irrigation of nearby fields and can be viewed from the bottom of the car park and picnic area on the site of Tattershall Station.

Dogdyke

A small community but in the past a busy water and rail transport centre. The Buccaneer restaurant and Hornblower's pub have modern names, but the Packet Inn is a reminder of the popular packet-boats which used to call here on their trips up and down the Witham. On the far bank Ferry Farm is another reminder of life here in the past.

Now there is only a small marina hidden behind the pubs.

Navigation

The Horncastle Canal is un-navigable apart from a few yards at its junction with the River Witham at Dogdyke, giving access to Belle Isle Marina.

Hornblower's pub and restaurant
See page 51.

Walking

There is no continuous path along the Horncastle Canal.

It is a pleasant route beside the River Bain from Tattershall Castle to the remains of Coningsby Lock.

Gibson's Cut—no footpath.

Bed & Breakfast at Tattershall village green.

There is no towpath on the River Bain from Tattershall to Dogdyke, despite being shown on OS maps.

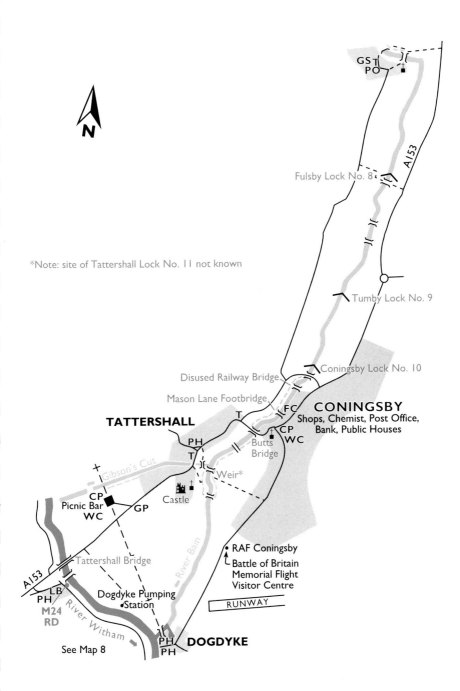

N

GS T
PO

A153

Fulsby Lock No. 8

Tumby Lock No. 9

*Note: site of Tattershall Lock No. 11 not known

Coningsby Lock No. 10

Disused Railway Bridge

Mason Lane Footbridge

TATTERSHALL

T

FC

CONINGSBY
Shops, Chemist, Post Office,
Bank, Public Houses

PH

T

CP
WC

Butts
Bridge

Gibson's Cut

Weir*

CP
Picnic Bar
WC

GP

Castle

River Bain

RAF Coningsby
Battle of Britain
Memorial Flight
Visitor Centre

Tattershall Bridge

A153

RUNWAY

LB
PH

M24
RD

River Witham

Dogdyke Pumping
Station

PH
PH

DOGDYKE

See Map 8

85

On the Wash, awaiting the tide to enter the River Witham © *Christine Potter*

Navigating the Wash

Crossing the Wash is not a passage to be undertaken lightly by those unfamiliar with the area's fickle weather and mobile sandbanks. It is strongly recommended that an experienced pilot is employed by all small craft.

Narrowboats are out of their element and crews of such craft must, therefore, seek expert assistance. British Waterways consider it to be a risky venture and will ask narrowboat masters to sign an indemnity form before passage through Boston Lock.

Boston Grand Sluice Lock

British Waterways controlled, dimensions on page 12. The lock is quite short but it is common practice to allow craft through when the water levels on each side of the lock are level, thereby negating the lock's lack of length.

Between 1st April and 31st October BW require 24hrs notice of passage. Between 1st November and 31st March, 48hrs notice is required.

It may be possible to contact Pilots via Boston Marina, or Fox Boats of March (Telephone, see page 94)

However, the Wash is used by some narrowboats as a direct route between the rivers Witham, Great Ouse, Nene and Welland. If the journey is to be undertaken it needs extensive planning.

From Boston to the open Wash is 6 nautical miles, and as an example the journey to the Great Ouse is approximately 30 miles of tidal water.

June, July, and August are usually the best months. Follow the pilot's orders but in general terms it would be advisable for a craft to have the following—lifejackets for every person on board, VHF radio and someone who knows how to use it properly, flares, echo-sounder, *up-to-date charts* (essential), an anchor with 300+ft warp, navigation lights, complete service overhaul on the engine, adequate fuel, and insurance cover for use in coastal waters. An echo-sounder is not essential but it is a fore-warning of problems. *Sheeting-down is recommended for the fore-deck,* and also surrounding the stern to give more free-board. The bigger the engine the better, in ratio to its weight. All tanks full, level trim is a must. *Narrowboats are much more stable when lashed together in pairs.*

Allocate more time than you think. The weather is fickle in the Wash and it has to be just right for a narrowboat to be safe. A pilot will not sail unless the weather, especially the wind, is acceptable, and the visibility adequate.

If you do the journey once, do not think that it will be the same a second time. The sands in the Wash move all the time, that is why **the very latest Admiralty chart is essential,** not one purchased months in advance. They are available from Boston Marina. A second useful publication is Symbols and Abbreviations used on Admiralty Charts. (published by the Admiralty and available from their official outlets).

The times in tide-tables are a rough guide. Every tide there are four hours when the sea is higher than the Witham.

It all sounds daunting, but small craft and narrowboats do cross the Wash successfully by making thorough preparations and employing a pilot. **Take short-cuts—geographical or financial—and you will endanger yourself, your crew, and your boat.**

Marine Safety Agency—Warning Notice
Locking-in Through Boston Grand Sluice
Those intending to go to The Wash are advised to consider the following points when planning their return to the River Witham.

- The time when there will be sufficient depth of water in The Haven to safely proceed up river to the Grand Sluice.

- An estimation of the length of time it will take for a particular boat to traverse the length of The Haven, given the anticipated flood tide to arrive at the Grand Sluice lock at the required time.

- The time when there will be sufficient tide for the Grand Sluice lock to be operated for passing through into the non-tidal River Witham, and the predicted period during which locking through will be permissible.

The reason for this Warning Notice is that there have been instances in the past of unsafe practices by some boaters, causing grounding and collisions owing to an unnecessary scramble to lock-through for the return transit to the non-tidal River Witham.

Navigating the River Trent

The route to the Fossdyke & Witham Navigations for inland waterway craft is via the tidal River Trent. Craft from the midlands and south will approach via Nottingham and Newark, the river becoming tidal below Cromwell Lock. From the north-east waterways, entry onto the tidal Trent is further downstream at Keadby Lock on the Stainforth & Keadby Canal. (See *The Complete Guide to the Sheffield & South Yorkshire Navigation*, in this series).

From Cromwell

Many narrowboats and small cruisers make the journey from Cromwell to Torksey each year. The tidal Trent should be regarded as an exciting challenge and there is little to fear so long as a vessel is properly prepared and the advice of the lock-keepers heeded. The 16-mile journey will take around three hours and it should be noted that the only place at which it is possible to stop or moor is the floating pontoon mooring at Dunham Bridge, 12 miles from Cromwell.

Craft must be reliable and should carry an effective anchor and cable. Buoyancy-aids are recommended, especially for children.

Look out for the large gravel-barges and know your horn signals.

The Cromwell lock-keeper will advise you of suitable times to commence your journey, and it is a good idea to telephone a couple of days beforehand. There is no point in trying to push against the incoming tide, so the lock-keeper will recommend your departure at high water, or up to seven hours later so as to reach Torksey before the following tide.

The river is surprisingly shallow towards low water, so do not cut corners on bends, and look out for navigation signs marking the channel in a couple of places. Better still, buy a copy of the *Tidal Trent Charts* from the Trent Boating Association (see page 94).

At Torksey, the lock is in a side-cut out of the tidal flow. There are floating pontoon moorings which can be used whilst waiting to use the lock.

From Keadby

The journey is 27 miles and will take an inland cruiser or narrowboat between three and six hours, depending on the speed of the tide. There is nowhere to moor en-route, but the journey could be broken at West Stockwith, 13 miles from Keadby, by locking into the Chesterfield Canal. (See *The Walkers' & Boaters' Guide to the Chesterfield Canal and Cuckoo Way*, in this series).

Telephone the Keadby lock-keeper 48 hours in advance to discuss your departure time. The intention is to leave Keadby as soon as possible on the flood, using the tide to speed progress up-river, and to arrive at Torksey before high-water.

As noted above, craft must be reliable and carry an effective anchor. Buoyancy-aids should be worn.

Look out for larger craft; gravel barges are common and coasters occasionally operate as far as Gainsborough. Remember that large vessels need the deep channel and can move very quickly: try to meet them on a straight section, move over to one side and stay there. Do not dart about undecided. Know the horn signals.

Port of Gainsborough Island Trophy Race

The Trent, Fossdyke and Witham are part of the course of the race colloquially known as POGIT. It is for yachts and they must sail, with penalties given for using engines.

The race proves part of Lincolnshire is an island. They start at Gainsborough, go down the Trent, down the Humber, down the coast to the Wash, up the Witham, along the Fossdyke, and down the Trent to Gainsborough. Organised by West Stockwith Yacht Club. (Telephone, see page 94).

**River Trent Navigation Facts
see page 90**

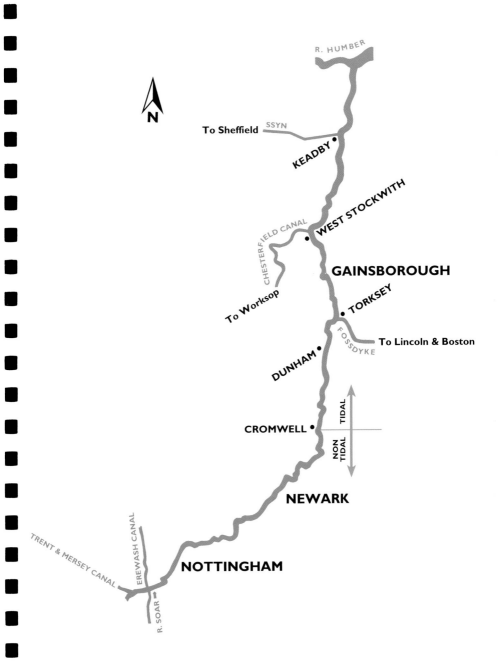

R. HUMBER

To Sheffield · SSYN

KEADBY

WEST STOCKWITH

CHESTERFIELD CANAL

To Worksop

GAINSBOROUGH

TORKSEY

To Lincoln & Boston

FOSSDYKE

DUNHAM

CROMWELL

TIDAL

NON TIDAL

NEWARK

TRENT & MERSEY CANAL

EREWASH CANAL

NOTTINGHAM

R. SOAR

River Trent Navigation Facts

Tide Terms:

Ebb Tide: When the river is running out towards the sea.

Flood: When the tide stops ebbing and turns to come back in.

Flood Tide (or flow): Tide running inland from the sea. Occasionally the tide is preceded by an Aegre, a wave like the Severn bore. It only forms on the largest tides and is ineffective between Torksey and Cromwell.

High Water: Tide stops running in.

Slack: Approximately ten minutes of still water at the top of the tide before the water starts running out again (ebbing).

Spring Tides: Twice a month, tides that rise to the highest of high water levels.

Neap Tides: The smallest tides.

Tide Tables and Aegre Schedule

Tide tables are available from the Environment Agency at Gainsborough (see page 94) or from British Waterways Office at Newark, most tidal locks and some chandleries.

The Environment Agency also produces a free Aegre schedule each year.

Trent Charts

Separate charts of *The Tidal Trent*, *The Non-Tidal Trent between Nottingham and Cromwell*, and the *Tidal River Ouse* are all available from the Trent Boating Association (see page 94).

VHF Radio

All the tidal locks monitor VHF Marine-Band Radio on channel 74.

(For Lock telephone numbers, see page 94).

Horn Signals

1 long blast	I am turning to starboard (right).
2 long blasts	I am turning to port (left).
3 long blasts	My engine is going astern.

Entering Torksey Cut and the Fossdyke from the River Trent

Public Transport

Lincolnshire County Council operates a very useful public transport information line, covering all rail and bus operators in the county. The Hotline number is 01522 553135.

Buses

Lincolnshire Road Car Ltd is the largest bus operator in the county and runs services throughout the area of this guide. However, there are smaller companies which may offer more frequent services on a local basis.

Slea Navigation, and Horncastle Canal.
For those walking the un-navigable parts of these waterways—there is a bus service Sleaford–Anwick and Tattershall Bridge–Horncastle.

Timetable details for all operators are available from the Hotline number above.

Lincoln Sightseeing

Open-top, double-decker. One hour, with commentary. More details on page 26.
Lincolnshire Road Car Ltd.
PO Box 15, St Mark Street
Lincoln LN5 7BB
Tel: 01522 522255.

Rail

There are rail stations at Saxilby, Lincoln, Sleaford and Boston.

Main-line connections. Services run from Sheffield and Doncaster to Saxilby and Lincoln, change for Sleaford and Boston.

Direct services to Sleaford and Boston go from Peterborough, Newark, and Grantham. Details from the Hotline number above.

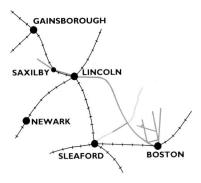

Rail Services:

Doncaster–Gainsborough–Lincoln–Sleaford–Spalding–Peterborough

Sheffield–Retford–Gainsborough–Lincoln

Coventry–Leicester–Nottingham–Newark–Lincoln–Market Rasen–Cleethorpes

Crewe–Nottingham–Grantham–Sleaford–Boston–Skegness

Public Houses

Map	Location	Distance from canal (yards)	Pub Name	Telephone	Meals	Children	Beer Garden	B + B
1	Torksey Lock	200	White Swan	01427 718653	L/E	✔	✔	No
1	Torksey Lock	800	Hume Arms	01427 718594	L/E	✔	✔	✔
1	Saxilby Moor	50	Pike House Inn	01522 702202	L/E	No	No	No
1	Saxilby		Bridge Inn	01522 702266	L/E	✔	✔	No
1	Saxilby		Ship	01522 702259	L	No	✔	No
1	Saxilby		Sun	01522 702326	L/E	✔	✔	No
2	Burton Lane End		The Woodcocks	01522 703460	L/E	✔	✔	No
2	Saxilby Road		The Pyewipe Inn	01522 528708	L/E	✔	✔	No
3	Brayford Pool		The Barge on the Brayford	01522 511448	L/E	✔	✔	No
3	Brayford Pool		Royal William IV	01522 528159	L/E	✔	✔	No
3	Lincoln		Witch & Wardrobe	01522 538114	L	✔	✔	No
3	Lincoln		The Green Dragon	01522 524950	L	✔	✔	No
3	Washingborough	700	Ferry Boat Inn	01522 790220	L/E	✔	✔	No
3	Washingborough	700	Hunter's Leap	01522 790458	No	No	No	No
3	Washingborough	700	Royal Oak	01522 794412	No	✔	✔	No
4	Five Mile Bridge	1300	Carpenters Arms	01522 751806	L/E	✔	No	No
4	Short Ferry		Tyrwhitt Arms	01526 398460	L/E	✔	✔	No
5	Bardney Bridge	200	Gypsey Queen	01526 397188	L/E	✔	✔	No
5	Bardney Bridge	1000	Nag's Head	01526 398402	L/E	No	✔	No
5	Bardney Bridge	1000	Bard's Family Pub	01526 398376	L/E	✔	✔	No
5	Bardney Bridge	1000	Black Horse	01526 398900	L/E	✔	✔	✔
5/6	Dunston Fen		White Horse Inn	01526 398341	L/E	✔	✔	✔
5/6	Southrey	100	Riverside Inn	01526 398374	L/E	✔	✔	✔
6/7	Kirkstead Bridge	200	Railway Hotel	01526 352580	L/E	✔	No	✔
6/7	Kirkstead Bridge	400	Kings Arms	01526 352633	L/E	✔	✔	✔
7/8	Tattershall Bridge		Royal Oak	01526 342413	L/E	✔	No	✔

Map	Location	Distance from canal (yards)	Pub Name	Telephone	Meals	Children	Beer Garden	B + B
8	Dogdyke		Hornblowers	01526 342124	L/E	✔	✔	No
8	Dogdyke		The Packet Inn	01526 342294	L/E	✔	✔	No
8	Chapel Hill		Orchard Caravans	01526 342414	L/E	✔	✔	✔
8	Chapel Hill	300	The Village Inn		‡	‡	‡	‡
9/10	Langrick Bridge	150	The Ferryboat Inn	01205 280273	L/E	✔	✔	No
10	Anton's Gowt Lock	100	The Oak Tree Inn	01205 360369	L/E	✔	✔	No
10	Boston Marina		Witham Tavern	01205 355570	L/E	✔	✔	No
11	South Kyme	100	Hume Arms	01526 861004	L/E	✔	✔	No
13	Haltham	400	Marmion Arms	01507 568326	L/E	✔	✔	No
13	Kirkby on Bain	100	Ebrington Arms	01526 352646	L/E	✔	✔	✔
14	Coningsby		Black Swan	01526 342481	L/E	✔	✔	✔
14	Coningsby		Castle Inn	01526 342336	L/E	✔	✔	✔
14	Coningsby		White Bull	01526 342439	L/E	✔	✔	✔
14	Coningsby		Ratty's Riverside Inn	01526 344609	L/E	✔	✔	No
14	Tattershall		Fortescue Arms	01526 342364	L/E	✔	✔	✔
Navigable Drains								
	Cowbridge		Cowbridge House Inn	01205 362597	L/E	✔	✔	No
	Boston		Ropers' Arms	01205 355741	No	✔	✔	No
	Boston		King William IV	01205 361640	L/E	✔	✔	No
	Boston		The Kings Arms	01205 364296	L/E	✔	✔	✔
	Sibsey	1000	White Hart	01205 750715	L/E	✔	✔	No
	Northlands	600	The Star Inn	01205 750362	L/E	✔	No	No
	Medlam Bridge	1400	Royal Oak	01205 480296	L/E	✔	✔	No
	Bunkers Hill Tunnel		The Olde Union Inn	01526 344011	L/E	✔	✔	✔

Key — Meals: **L** = Lunchtime; **E** = Evenings. Children: ✔ = Children welcome;
‡ Closed at the time of writing.

N.B. Facilities provided by pubs are liable to change—it is recommended to phone in advance.

Further Information

British Waterways

Newark Office   01636 704481

Fossdyke
Torksey Lock   01427 718202

River Witham
Boston Lock (Grand Sluice)   01205 364864

River Trent
Keadby Lock   01724 782205
West Stockwith Lock   01427 890204
Cromwell Lock   01636 821213

Inland Waterways Groups

Inland Waterways Association
    (Lincoln Branch)   01469 530138
Sleaford Navigation Society   01522 689460

Boating Contacts

Belle Isle Marina, Dogdyke   01526 342124
Boston Marina   01205 364420
Environment Agency, (Trent)   01427 612205
    Corringham Road,
    Gainsborough DN21 1QH.
Fox Boats, of March, Cambs.   01354 52770
Lincoln Canoe Club   01522 685479
Lincoln Marina   01522 526896
Lincoln, Brayford Pool
    Harbourmaster   01522 521452
Orchard Caravans   01526 342414
Port of Boston   01205 365571
Trent Boating Association
    78 Old Retford Road,
    Sheffield S13 9RA.
West Stockwith Yacht Club   01427 890673
Witham Fourth
    Internal Drainage Board.   01205 310099
    47 Norfolk Street,
    Boston PE21 6PP.
    Foreman   01205 353758

Trip Boats

Lincoln, Brayford Pool
    City of Lincoln,
    April to September   (day) 01522 546853
                   (evening) 01909 483111
Lincolnshire Narrowboat Trust   01522 720975
Boston
    Adventure Afloat   01205 871439
    Maritime Leisure Cruises   01205 460595
                   or 0374 798932

Hire Boats

Lincolnshire Narrow Boats   01522 702947

Angling

Boston Angling Association	01205 350088
Horncastle Angling Club	01507 527277
Lincoln & District	
Angling Association	01522 722781
Witham & District	
Joint Angling Federation	01472 690782

RAF Heritage

Battle of Britain Memorial Flight   01526 344041
Lincoln Cathedral
(The Airmen's Chapel
of St. Michael)   01522 544544
Details of the many RAF museums, sites,
airfields, aviation trails, in the county from
Lincolnshire Tourism (see opposite).

Windmills

Ellis' Mill, Lincoln	01522 523870
Maud Foster, Boston	01205 352188
Sibsey Trader	01246 822621

Maps

Ordnance Survey:
Landranger Series,
maps 121, 122, 130, 131

General

Boston.	
Guildhall Museum.	01205 365954
St Botolph's (The Stump)	01205 362859
Dogdyke Pumping Station	01526 342352
Lincoln	
Castle	01522 511068
Cathedral	01522 544544
Tour Bus	01522 522255
Incredibly Fantastic	
Old Toy Show	01522 520534
The Lawn	01522 560330
Theatre Royal	01522 525555
Usher Art Gallery	01522 527980
Lincolnshire Trust for Nature	
Conservation	01507 526667
Sleaford	
Cogglesford Mill	01529 414294
Tattershall Castle	
National Trust	01526 342543

Tourist Information

Boston	01205 356656
Gainsborough	01427 615411
Horncastle. Easter—Sept.	01507 526636
Lincoln	01522 529828
	or 01522 512971
Lincolnshire County Council,	
Recreational Services	01522 552222
Lincolnshire Tourism	01522 526450
Sleaford	01529 414294
Woodhall Spa. Easter—Sept.	01526 353775

Further Reading

Richardson, Christine, *Water Ways*
The Hallamshire Press, 1995, ISBN 1-874718-08-3
(Where to find twenty-two rivers and canals in
eastern England.)
Clarke, J N, *The Horncastle and Tattershall Canal*
Oakwood Press, 1990, ISBN 0-85361-398-2.
(History of the named waterway.)
Other Richlow Guides
by Christine Richardson and John Lower,
from The Hallamshire Press, Sheffield

*The Complete Guide to the Sheffield & South Yorkshire
Navigation*, 1995, ISBN 1-874718-07-5
*A Walkers' and Boaters' Guide to the Chesterfield Canal
and Cuckoo Way*, 1994, ISBN 1-874718-25-3

Index